LET N
HEART BE TROUBLED

LET NOT YOUR
HEART BE TROUBLED

Martyn Lloyd-Jones

Foreword by
Elizabeth Catherwood and Ann Beatt

CROSSWAY BOOKS
WHEATON, ILLINOIS

Let Not Your Heart Be Troubled

Copyright © 2009 by Elizabeth Catherwood and Ann Beatt

Originally published as *Be Still My Soul: Resting in the Greatness of God and His Love for You*, copyright © 1995; published by Servant Publications.

Published by Crossway Books
    a publishing ministry of Good News Publishers
    1300 Crescent Street
    Wheaton, Illinois 60187

Cover design: Cindy Kiple

Cover photo: Getty Images

First printing, 2009

Printed in the United States of America

All Scripture quotations are taken from the King James Version of the Bible.

Tradepaperback ISBN: 978-1-4335-0119-7

PDF ISBN: 978-1-4335-1245-2

Mobipocket ISBN: 978-1-4335-1246-9

Library of Congress Cataloging-in-Publication Data
Lloyd-Jones, David Martyn.
  (Be still my soul)
  Let not your heart be troubled / Martyn Lloyd-Jones ; foreword by Elizabeth Catherwood and Ann Beatt.
    p. cm.
  Originally published: Be still my soul. Ann Arbor, Mich. : Vine Books, c1995.
  Includes bibliographical references.
  ISBN 978-1-4335-0119-7 (tpb)
  1. Trust in God—Christianity—Sermons. 2. Peace of mind—Religious aspects—Christianity—Sermons. 3. Sermons, English. I. Title.
BV4637.L55   2009
252'.058—dc22   2009000678

VP		18	17	16	15	14	13	12	11	10	09
14	13	12	11	10	9	8	7	6	5	4	3	2	1

CONTENTS

FOREWORD

Our father, Martyn Lloyd-Jones (1899–1981), preached these sermons in 1951 in Westminster Chapel in London. These were difficult times for the people of Britain, indeed for all the Western world. The Second World War was not long over, and many economic, political, national, and personal problems were left in its wake. But there was also the menace of the Cold War, with the nuclear threat that hung over both sides. There was not the same euphoria as there had been after the First World War; people were anxious and fearful.

So it was in this atmosphere that our father preached this short series of sermons. They were intended to comfort, strengthen, and build up Christians in their "most holy faith" (Jude 20) and to bring unbelievers to a knowledge of the only way in which men and women can face matters of life and death. He sought to show that these familiar words were not only relevant in funerals but could be applied to all facets of our lives, and the way in which he handled these words was characteristic of his ministry. He did not use them as a kind of soothing refrain that would lull our fears to rest. Rather, he went through them carefully, showing that the way to deal with our fears was first to confront them and recognize them and then to realize that the answer to them was only to be found in the great and unchanging truths of the Christian gospel.

So he shows what these truths are: belief in God, belief in Jesus Christ and his work, the certainty of his promise that he will take us safely to his Father's house, and so on. These are foundational doctrines, but he does not deal with them clinically. Throughout we are reminded of the love that brought it all to pass.

He once described preaching as "logic on fire," and this is evident in these sermons. They are perhaps briefer in their exposition than, for example, his later great series on Romans and Ephesians, but the truths and the spirit are the same.

Toward the end of his life, when he was very weak, he experienced for himself these things that he had preached earlier. One evening his doctor said to him, "I don't like to see you weary and worn and sad like this."

"No," came back the whispered answer, "not sad!" He pointed those of us in the family to the great verses in 2 Corinthians 4:16–18:

> For which cause we faint not; but though our outward man perish, yet the inward man is renewed day by day. For our light affliction, which is but for a moment, worketh for us a far more exceeding and eternal weight of glory; while we look not at the things which are seen, but at the things which are not seen: for the things which are seen are temporal; but the things which are not seen are eternal.

He also asked us not to pray for healing. "Don't try to hold me back from the glory," he said. He was ill for many months, but the great truths of John 14 held him fast. He knew that the Savior whom he had served so faithfully for so many years had prepared a place for him. He knew the quiet heart, the stillness of the soul, of which these sermons speak.

Elizabeth Catherwood
Ann Beatt
September 9, 1994

PART I

We Must Believe

Let not your heart be troubled:
ye believe in God, believe also in me.

JOHN 14:1

1

LET NOT YOUR HEART BE TROUBLED

Let not your heart be troubled: ye believe in God, believe
also in me.

JOHN 14:1

As we come to consider this great passage together, I think
most commentators agree that a better way of translating it
is, "Let not your heart be troubled, believe in God, believe also
in me." In other words, it is probably right to say that it is the
imperative that we have in both cases.

However, these words are probably familiar to most of us;
indeed they are perhaps some of the most familiar and tender
words ever uttered by our Lord and Savior Jesus Christ. They
are words, therefore, that we often tend to take without really
facing them and their true meaning and without analyzing them
as we should. It is to me a tragedy that so often we rob ourselves
of the actual message of some of the most glorious statements
in Scripture simply because we regard them as literature. We
are content with some general effect or influence that they may
produce upon us instead of taking the trouble to arrive at their
exact meaning and their precise import.

Now that, I think, is very true of these words, words that
may be most familiar to us in funerals. They are words of comfort and consolation, which we tend, therefore, to think of far

too often as some kind of beautiful music or some wonderful diction. So we never get any further, almost feeling at times that it is a sacrilege to analyze something that is so beautiful.

> Let not your heart be troubled: ye believe in God, believe also in me. In my Father's house are many mansions: if it were not so, I would have told you. I go to prepare a place for you. And if I go and prepare a place for you, I will come again, and receive you unto myself; that where I am, there ye may be also. . . . Peace I leave with you, my peace I give unto you. . . . Let not your heart be troubled, neither let it be afraid. (John 14:1–3, 27)

We have heard those words many times, but I wonder what would happen if we suddenly had to sit down with paper in front of us and face a question such as, state the doctrine contained in those familiar words—what exactly do they say? Have these words, I wonder, come to us merely in that general manner, that kind of general consolation, that can be done equally well by beautiful music or by any beautiful thoughts or passages of literature? Or have we derived comfort and consolation from them because we have realized the doctrine that they are announcing?

Our Lord's whole purpose in uttering these words was that he might instruct his disciples and help them by bringing them to a deeper knowledge and understanding of truth. He was addressing their minds primarily, and the way in which he came to do so is of significance and importance. He had just been telling these men, who had now accompanied him for about three years, that he was about to leave them. He was still young, in his early thirties, and to their astonishment and utter chagrin he announced that he was going to leave them. "Now," he said, "is the Son of man glorified, and God is glorified in him. . . . Little children, yet a little while I am with you. Ye shall seek me: and as I said unto the Jews, Whither I go, ye cannot come; so now I say to you" (John 13:31, 33). But he realized at once that this information had upset these disciples and had made them unhappy and disconsolate. Their hearts had become troubled, they were ill at ease, and they had lost their peace because they were suddenly confronted by a problem.

Now we need not go into detail as to why the disciples felt this so acutely; that has its interest and its importance, but we need not stay with it now. It might very well have been due to the fact that they had become overdependent upon him. They had never met anybody like him before. They had been ordinary men living ordinary lives in this world, having their ups and downs and problems, but suddenly they had met him and had been called by him to follow him and keep him company in a very special way, and it had been a marvelous and thrilling experience. His very personality was something quite apart and unique; they had never seen anybody like this before. There was something in his very person; to look into his eyes was to recognize something that they had never known.

Then it was amazing to hear his extraordinary teaching, his gracious words, his knowledge, his understanding; to see him performing miracles, cleansing lepers, making the lame walk, giving sight to the blind, even raising the dead; and thus, imperceptibly, they had become entirely dependent upon him. I suppose the temptation in such a situation was that they would not stop to think, they just relied utterly upon him; and then, suddenly, he announced that he was going away, and at once they were filled with a sense of alarm and concern. Did that mean that they would have to go back to where they were before? Did it mean a reversion to their hopeless kind of life? "How can we do without him?" they thought. "If he is going, then we are finished, we are undone." And our Lord recognized that they were thinking all this.

Or it may have been that they had recognized in him, rather vaguely and dimly, yet surely, the Messiah who was expected. They had their Jewish notions as to what the Messiah was to be and about the kingdom he was to establish, and it was largely political. They had been troubled because he had not set himself up as king; some had tried to force him to do so. They had decided to wait upon him, feeling that at some point not far removed he would declare himself. He would set himself up as king, make a great attack upon the Romans, and so rid them of the Roman tyranny and set up a wonderful kingdom. But here he was, announcing that he was going away! He had done nothing about bringing in the kingdom. So they were unhappy and had a feeling that they had been misled and somewhat deluded; he was not what they thought he was going to be.

Well, they no doubt had many such thoughts, but the important thing is that our Lord sensed all this in them. He saw that they had become disturbed and unhappy and that, above all, their trouble was in their hearts. Their hearts were "troubled," and so, in a very characteristic manner, he dealt with their troubles and administered to them this glorious word of consolation.

There is one other preliminary remark that I must make at this point: it is vital that we remember at what time in his life our Lord did this. It was on the very eve of the cross. He knew what was coming; he had been earlier on the Mount of Transfiguration, and there Moses and Elijah had spoken to him concerning "his decease which he should accomplish at Jerusalem" (Luke 9:31). He knew what was going to be involved on the cross; he knew he was being made sin for mankind. He knew that when God would lay on him the sins of us all, it would mean a terrible moment of separation from the face of God. He knew all that, and as he said later on in the garden of Gethsemane, his soul was "exceeding sorrowful" (Matthew 26:38); nevertheless he turned aside to comfort these unhappy followers of his. He was more concerned about their unhappiness than his own immediate problem, and thus we have this wonderful view that on the very eve of the cross, our Lord gave himself freely in comfort and consolation to others.

Bearing in his own body the sins of the world, he had sufficient compassion and love and sympathy and understanding to turn to the wretched man who was there being crucified with him.

How typical and characteristic of him! He did the same thing on the cross itself, you remember, even after they had driven the cruel nails into his hands and his feet. There, dying on the cross, he had time to speak to that thief dying by his side. Bearing in his own body the sins of the world, he had sufficient compassion and love and sympathy and understanding to turn to the wretched man who was there being crucified with him.

Now I emphasize all this at the beginning because whatever else we may or may not learn as we consider this passage, let us realize that the one about whom we are speaking, the one about whom we are concerned, is one like that. That is Jesus, the Savior, the Lord Jesus Christ whom we preach. He is the center of this New Testament message and gospel. He is the one who, though he is the Son of God himself, is ready and willing and able to meet us exactly where we are. He even takes the trouble to read our minds and thoughts in order to answer our questions before we ever ask them, and he gives us consolation before we even give expression to our need and unhappiness.

So as he said this to the disciples, he says it, of course, once and forever, to all others who at any time or in any age or in any place know this same condition of the troubled heart. Here in these three chapters, chapters 14, 15, and 16 of John's Gospel, our Lord administers this final comfort and consolation to all who feel overwhelmed and bewildered by the problems of life and of existence.

I suppose that in many ways it can truthfully be said that the greatest need of men and women in this world is the need of what is called a quiet heart, a heart at leisure from itself.

> *The greatest need of men and women in this world is the need of what is called a quiet heart.*

Is that not, in the last analysis, the thing for which we are all looking? You can if you like call it peace; that means exactly the same thing, peace of mind and peace of heart, tranquillity. We are all restless; we are all disturbed. There is unhappiness in us, and it is produced by many different causes.

One thing that causes all our hearts to be restless and disturbed, one thing that robs everybody of peace, is the thought of death. This is a great and certain fact; in the words of the woman of Tekoah, "For we must needs die, and are as water spilt on the ground, which cannot be gathered up again" (2 Samuel 14:14). That is a most disturbing, a most troubling thought. The author of the Epistle to the Hebrews says that until we become Christians, we are all in lifelong "bondage . . . through fear of death" (Hebrews 2:15). Shakespeare, who knew the human heart, gives these words to Hamlet: "The dread of something after death, the undiscovered country, from whose bourn no traveller returns."

"Conscience," he adds, "doth make cowards of us all." Yes, we do this and that, but thought of that "undiscovered country" upsets everything. That is the trouble and that is the cause of the restless, unquiet heart.

Then there are the problems that are incidental to life in this world, life and its almost inevitable ills that come sooner or later—illness, accident, disappointment, financial loss, trouble in business, the serious illness of a child or a loved one, the death of someone close to us. These are the things that come and test us all, and we cannot avoid them. We all want to make our plans for life and living. But when we think we have made our perfect plans, something suddenly happens, and our whole world begins to shake and to quake. Certain ills simply cannot be avoided, things that are bound to happen, the tragedies of life.

And all this is in addition to the particular problems of the current century. Every age of mankind has been subject to the things that I have mentioned, but on top of these things we have this uncertain world in which we are living, with all the possibility of wars and many other threats. The supreme problem is that of trying to face these things and to achieve a quiet heart. I think that any analysis of modern literature and of the conduct of the vast majority of people will indicate clearly that men and women are trying to achieve peace in some shape or form.

The claim of the gospel is not only that it can give us a
quiet heart, but also that nothing else can do it.

We need to determine what is really likely to give us this quiet heart. We must start by being realistic and by saying that it is not only the Christian gospel that offers us freedom from the troubled heart. There are many ways in which we are exhorted to try to find this peace. So I must start with the negative. I must deal with the false before I can come to the true because men and women who are holding on to false solutions and do not find satisfaction must come and listen to the gospel. The claim of the gospel is not only that it can give us a quiet heart, but also that nothing else can do it.

Of course, people do not like that sort of claim today; they say that it is "intolerant." We are living in days when people are always saying, "We want a world conference of all the religions, so we can all get together and pick out the best in each." But you cannot do that with the gospel of Jesus Christ. It is exclusive, and its challenge is that Christ, and Christ alone, can truly give us peace.

Now let me substantiate that by reminding you of some of the other ways in which it is suggested we can find this peace. One is that we should refuse to think. We must put that first because it is the most common. People say increasingly that if you are foolish enough to think in this world, then it is not surprising that you are unhappy, and in a sense you deserve to be so. They say that the whole trouble with men and women is that they persist in thinking; if only they had the sense to stop doing that and to be just like the animals and go back to nature and live the animal life, all would be well. That was the philosophy of D. H. Lawrence, who said that man has overdeveloped the higher part of his brain, but if only he would revert to the lower type of life, he would be much happier. Many say that, though not in such a philosophical way. "If you want to be happy," they say, "just get away from your troubles." So you fill up the agenda of your life as much as you can with meeting other people, going to entertainments, and many other things—in other words, *escapism*.

Another way in which we are told that we can achieve the quiet heart is to espouse and adopt the philosophy of what is called *optimism*, and it is astounding that there are still many who follow this philosophy. It takes many shapes and forms. Some still cling tenaciously to their belief in an inevitable kind of evolution to a better life. They say that the whole of mankind is gradually evolving to a higher state and a more perfect condition in which our troubles and problems will be left behind; and they still believe that in spite of all that has happened in the past one hundred years! Others do not put it exactly like that, but their optimism consists in saying, "It is all right; there are temporary setbacks, but things are going to get better." This happened before the Second World War; such people were quite sure, up to the last minute, that Hitler would embrace wisdom. This is belief in optimism for the sake of being optimistic. People are proud of this; they go on looking at the bright side of things and believe it is their duty to always smile, come what may. Many are trying to achieve the quiet heart in that way.

Then, going up the scale a little, we come to the next false hope, which is what I would call the philosophy of *fatalism*. I think this is becoming increasingly common. In its simplest form, it says, "What is to be will be; and all the thinking and all the worrying and all the calculating in the world cannot affect it. The trouble with people is that they persist in thinking, but if only they saw that to do that is to exaggerate the trouble, they would stop thinking and making themselves unhappy. It is because they go to meet their troubles and anticipate them that they are so troubled. But everything seems to be rigidly fixed by a fatalistic principle. Therefore do not think—just wait until things do happen and you will have a kind of temporary peace and an assuaging of your trouble." Many pacify themselves and think they can get true peace that way.

The next one is what I would call *the psychological method*. This is slightly different because it attempts a kind of positive and active treatment of us and of our minds. It is just a device to train us to play tricks with our own thoughts and hearts. In a sense, it is not interested in our problems; it is interested in our reaction to those problems. The psychologist is concerned with giving us peace of mind; that is his objective. The different types of psychological treatment all say the same thing to us: "Why worry?" They try to show us, in various ways, the folly of worrying. They tell us to try to think of beautiful and pleasant things; they say that we must deliberately subjugate our thoughts and project them onto other things and so on. So when people become agitated, they rush to a psychologist.

Then, still going up the scale, the next thing is the adopting of an attitude of resignation or *stoicism*. Or, as they prefer to call it today, "the scientific attitude" or "the psychological calm." Many people talk about this attitude. They say the one thing we must watch is our feelings. Our trouble is that we all tend to be controlled by our feelings, and if our feelings take over, then we become agitated and unhappy. So the solution to that, they say, is the adoption of this particular teaching. We must stand back and have a psychological calm; we must become scientists. There is nothing new about all that. The Stoics did it long ago; that was the very essence of their philosophy, that you must always keep a careful curb upon your feelings and emotions, otherwise they will cripple you. So you must take yourself in hand and control your emotions, and you must say to yourself, "I must be objective. I must be scientific. I must not let myself be immersed in these things."

And that brings me to the last philosophy, the one that is provided by cults and other religions like Christian Science, which deliberately set out to give people freedom from trouble and worry, a kind of perfect calm in spite of everything. Other cults try to do the same thing. I refer to "the cults of other religions" because there is a remarkable increase in the number of such religions today, chiefly coming from the East, that offer this escape from trouble and the way to a quiet heart. There is a new interest in Buddhism and Hinduism and things of that kind. (It is very interesting to notice that it is some of the men who used to call themselves intellectuals who are turning to Buddhism and to these Eastern religions and various forms of mysticism. They have tried to face their problems, and they have failed. So they have come to the conclusion that their only salvation is in *mysticism*, going into the heart of the universe, losing themselves in the spirit that is at the back of everything.) Many are seeking this quiet heart and deliverance from their troubles in that way.

I am always so sorry for "the bright young things."
The actual truth about them is that they are so afraid of
life that they dare not think about it.

Now obviously we cannot deal with all these things now, but I want to say that general comments can be made about them all. It seems to me, first, that they are, all of them, in the last analysis pessimistic and hopeless. To refuse to think is to be profoundly pessimistic; that is why I am always so sorry for "the bright young things," the people who live for pleasure and say, "How happy we are by contrast with you miserable Christians!" But the actual truth about them is that they are so afraid of life that they dare not think about it. That is the most profound pessimism that I know.

It is exactly the same with the pathetic optimism that refuses to face the facts that are confronting us today. There is no evidence that man as man is progressing and evolving. It is the same with fatalism, which is utterly hopeless. It says, "What is the use of anything? Things are just going to happen; therefore do nothing about them, and do not even think about them."

It is the same with resignation. Resignation says, "Things

are going to be like this, so I just have to put up with them somehow." That again is hopelessness. Psychology, as I have said, does not face the problem; it plays tricks with itself. It is like whistling in the dark, and the same applies to the cults and these various other religions. You may have to be reincarnated many times, we are told, but your hope is that you will eventually become merged into the universe. That, too, is profound pessimism. So all these views, at their very best and highest, are devised just to help us get through. They simply help us postpone our problems, they do not solve them; and none of them can give us real joy or satisfaction.

All these views simply help us postpone our problems,
they do not solve them; and none of them
can give us real joy.

But I suppose the greatest criticism of them is that they, all of them in a sense, leave the problem up to the individual. How true this is of the Eastern religions! You will find that they leave it up to us. We will each have to go through terrible ordeals; we will have to discipline our body, mind, and every part of ourselves. They ask us to deliver ourselves in some shape or form, and thus they leave us with the problem. To me it is very significant that the people who are turning to Buddhism are, as I have said, the so-called "intellectuals." You have to be an intellectual before you can go in for such things because they leave it all up to you, and it takes a lot of thinking time to employ these methods of attaining peace. They have nothing whatever to give to the ordinary person. They have nothing to give those who are so busy with their jobs, their families, their homes, and various other things that they cannot read these wonderful philosophical ideas. Ordinary people have no time to go through these long processes of discipline and prayer. Eastern religions have nothing to give such people.

The trouble I find with psychology is that it is simply an attempt to give you quiet nerves instead of giving you a quiet heart. I want to be fair to psychology. It can give us, up to a point, quiet nerves, but that is not what we need—we need a quiet heart. Thank God for something that, as far as it goes, can give us quiet nerves, but do you want to be at rest on the surface or do you want to be at rest in the very depths and vitals of your being? It is at that point that the gospel claims that it, and it alone, can meet and satisfy our deepest need, and here in John 14 we are told exactly how it does that.

I am simply introducing this subject now; we shall go on to consider it in detail, but let me just give you an outline of it. Here is something authoritative, something from Someone who has given us the truth from the dawn of history. Here is something that worked in these particular disciples to whom he was speaking. Here were men who, having listened to this gospel and having proved it in their lives, were able to face the whole might and tyranny of the Roman Empire, with all its cruel persecutions, who were more than conquerors, triumphing and rejoicing. Read the great story of the apostles and the martyrs and the first confessors. It has worked, and it continues to work.

We must make other certain general statements also. What seems to me to be so entirely different about the gospel, at the very beginning, is that it always faces facts, it is always realistic, it never conceals anything. Read these chapters of John's Gospel, and you will find that our Lord brought these men face-to-face with the very worst, whereas all the other teachings and philosophies try to hide the worst from us. My heart will not be really quiet until I have been told the very worst and faced it, and then I can surmount it. I do not believe in a teaching that simply plays tricks with me. I have no use for a philosophy that tells me there is no such thing as matter, and because of that there can be no pain, and therefore I do not have pain—when I know there is pain. I know that may work psychologically; it may convince me for a time—I believe the lie and am relieved. But I do not merely want to be relieved of my pain. I want the disease to be faced and tackled.

The gospel commends itself to me because of its truth, because it does not just say, "Well now, let's forget our troubles and think of something beautiful." It says, "In the world ye shall have tribulation" (John 16:33). It says that in a world like this, dominated by Satan, there will be "wars and rumours of wars" (Matthew 24:6). It is psychology and not the gospel that just tries to make us forget our troubles for the time being. The gospel of Jesus Christ always, therefore, of necessity annoys certain people, people who think that a place of worship is just a place where you listen to beautiful things, and therefore while you are sitting there, you forget your problems and the problems of the world—these people are certain to be annoyed.

Our Lord brought these men face-to-face with the very worst, whereas all the other teachings and philosophies try to hide the worst from us.

The gospel confronts us with facts. It is all based upon a person; it is based upon certain things that happened historically. It comes and tells me, "Let not your heart be troubled." But it comes in the light of Gethsemane and Jesus' trial and cruel death upon the cross, the broken body, the burial, the utter hopelessness and despair. Then, and only then, it goes on to tell me of the Resurrection and the glory of the Ascension and the sending of the Holy Spirit, and that puts me in an entirely different position.

It has taken me through the facts, through the tunnel of darkness to the dawn that lights the other end.

Moreover, it commends itself to me because it gives me an explanation and satisfies my mind. The gospel has given this philosophy of history. It not only gives me the facts, it explains them; it puts them into a coherent whole. There is a great view of life in the Bible—we shall deal with that later. I am not finally helped by being told, for example, "It is all right, do not think about it, you will die and come back in some other form. You will go through a series of incarnations, and you will finally get lost in the vast universe." I do not believe that the whole trouble is my physical flesh. I know that the trouble is in my spirit. So I must have something that satisfies my mind. I want to face life; I want an explanation of why it is in the position that it is, and I have the explanation here and only here.

> *I do not believe that the whole trouble is my physical*
> *flesh. I know that the trouble is in my spirit.*

And the thing that commends itself most of all to me is that it does not leave it all to me, but it links all to the power of God. "Let not your heart be troubled"—why? "Believe in God, believe also in me," says Christ; in other words, "Trust me." I have mentioned those who spend long, weary hours in all the details of a busy everyday life; they cannot follow "the mystic way." What can I offer them? If I do not have a gospel that can give them a quiet heart, I have no gospel worthy of the name. But thank God, I do have a gospel for them. I have a gospel that tells them that the one who walked through this world and triumphed over it, even over death and the grave itself, has said, "At that day ye shall know that I am in my Father, and ye in me, and I in you" (John 14:20), so that into their unutterable weakness comes the might and the power of the Son of God who has vanquished death and the grave, and against him nothing and no one can finally stand.

"Let not your heart be troubled . . . believe in God." Yes, believe in God, the God of the Old Testament, the God of the promises, the God of the covenants, the God of whom it is said, "When my father and my mother forsake me, then the LORD will take me up" (Psalm 27:10). This is the same God who told mankind from the beginning that his desire was to bless them, to give them peace and joy, and to have them as his children. Trust him. Yes, but so often that is the difficulty, is it not? It is all here in John 14. Philip, one of the disciples, said to our Lord in effect, "If only we knew the Father, it would suffice us, but the difficulty is knowing that God in heaven is our Father." And our Lord's reply is, "Have I been so long time with you, and yet hast thou not known me, Philip?" (vv. 8–9). "Believe in God, believe also in me," he says, "because without believing in me, you will never really know the Father."

Thomas, too, had a problem: "We don't know this 'way' you are talking about," he said in essence. And our Lord's great answer to him was, "I am the way, the truth, and the life: no man cometh unto the Father, but by me" (vv. 5–6). And speaking about prayer—and how often we find difficulty in this—he said in summary, "It is all right—I am going to be with the Father. If you ask anything in my name, I will do it" (v. 14).

But then we say, "We are so weak. How can we go through with it in a world like this?" He says, "I will not leave you comfortless" (v. 18), which translated means, "I will not leave you orphans." And he adds that he will "give [us] another Comforter" (v. 16). This is the blessed doctrine of the gift of the Holy Spirit, who comes and dwells within us and reveals and explains things and energizes and empowers and enables us.

*The Holy Spirit dwells within us and reveals and
explains things and energizes and empowers
and enables us.*

It is all here in John's Gospel. But let me summarize it all so that you may be encouraged. There has been one in this world called Jesus of Nazareth, and it is he who says to you, "Let not your heart be troubled . . . believe in me," which means, "Come to me, tell me your troubles, tell me all about your difficulty about God, the difficulty of prayer, the difficulty about your weak will and failure."

I do not care what it is that makes you restless and ill at ease. It may be the possibility of war, it may be illness, it may be business troubles, it may be your own weakness morally in the realm of the will—whatever it is, whatever is troubling and making you unhappy, go to him about it. He is the one who loved you enough to die for you. He said, "Come unto me, all ye that labour and are heavy laden, and I will give you rest" (Matthew 11:28). There is no need for you to be unhappy and restless. Believe in God. Believe in the Son of God, the Lord Jesus Christ who came on earth to deliver you from that very thing and who has removed every barrier between you and God and who can give you rest and peace here and now.

2

BELIEVE IN GOD

Thus saith the LORD the King of Israel, and his redeemer
the LORD of hosts; I am the first, and I am the last; and be-
side me there is no God.

ISAIAH 44:6

We have been considering together why our Lord spoke
the words recorded in John 14:1, "Let not your heart
be troubled . . . believe in God, believe also in me." He spoke
them primarily, you remember, in order to comfort his disciples
to whom he had just made the announcement that he was going
to leave them. They were disappointed, and they were unhappy,
and they were afraid as they thought about the future. So it was
to deal with this that our Lord spoke as he did, and these are not
only words of comfort and consolation to those to whom they
were first spoken—they have a message that is as true today
in this modern world of ours as it was then. Furthermore, as I
have been emphasizing, here is a tried method, something that
worked in these very disciples. You will recall that the effect of
the most violent persecution upon them was just to make them
meet together in a prayer meeting to thank God that they had
been counted worthy to suffer for his name's sake.

So in light of that, we have begun to discuss the whole question of how we may obtain a quiet heart. We have considered
some of the false methods that are suggested to us, and we have
realized that they do not meet the problem at all. So, having

begun to look at our Lord's method, we now come to consider a little more in detail what this method is; and here he summarizes it all in this one statement: "Let not your heart be troubled." But how are we to avoid that? The answer is, "Believe in God, believe also in me."

The first thing, then, is to
believe in God.

The first thing, then, is to believe in God. This is always the starting point, the key to the understanding of the biblical method of giving mankind a quiet heart. It can never be said too frequently that the Bible is not concerned primarily to give us a quiet heart; its interest is something else. Its primary concern is something that is infinitely more important, and unless we understand its purpose and understand that it is of the very essence of what we may call the biblical method, we shall go hopelessly astray. The trouble with us is that we always tend to aim at these things directly; we always look for some immediate consolation, some immediate comfort.

Of course, this is true of us in every realm and department. I always feel this can be best illustrated by using the physical analogy. A man who is taken ill is generally not interested in his disease as such; what he is interested in is, of course, the suffering that he has to endure because of the illness. He may have a pain, or he may be short of breath or something else, but the interest of the patient is invariably in his symptoms. What he wants is something to relieve them. I admit that this is perfectly natural, and there is nothing wrong in desiring to be free from pain; there is no merit in suffering it. But I must emphasize here that the Bible teaches us that we must not only be concerned with the relief of the pain.

Anything that merely gives us relief from unpleasant
symptoms is not enough. What we should always be
interested in, in every realm, is health.

A man who sins suffers remorse; he has agony of mind, and
the one thing he wants is to get rid of that agony. But what he
really needs is much more than immediate comfort. Anything
that merely gives us relief from the unpleasant symptoms of our
disease or from our agony of mind is not enough. In fact, it is
doing us a very grave disservice, for what we should always be
interested in, in every realm, is health. That is the thing to aim
at—not merely an absence of trouble but the positive condition
of health.

Now it is at this point that we come across what is the great
differentiating and characteristic feature of the Bible and its
method. You see, nearly all these other methods that are being
offered to us today are simply concerned to give us immediate
relief from pain. They are all drugs in some shape or form; they
have just that one interest—to relieve us. And many people come
to God and to God's house in that kind of way, expecting to have
some temporary relief of pain, something that can make them
happy. But the Bible teaches us that happiness and joy and peace
and the absence of pain and trouble are always by-products; they
are always the result of something else. They are not something
the Bible gives us directly. They always follow something else
that has gone before.

The classic statement of this was made by our Lord in his
Sermon on the Mount, when he said, "Blessed are they which
do hunger and thirst after"—happiness, joy, peace? Not at all—
"blessed are they which do hunger and thirst after *righteousness*:
for they shall be filled" (Matthew 5:6, emphasis added). In other
words, if you make happiness or joy or peace your one aim and

object in life, it is certain you will never find it; but if you put righteousness as your main aim, and if you become so concerned about righteousness and true living that you can be said to be hungering and thirsting after it, well then, says our Lord, you will be filled with happiness. It will follow.

This, I think you will agree with me, is something that is absolutely vital and fundamental. If you come to the Christian faith merely because of what you want it to do, you will never get that thing, nor will you get anything else. The Bible must be taken in its own way; it must be accepted on its own terms. There are no shortcuts once you begin to deal with God. God demands something that is central from us—he demands total allegiance. You cannot take things out of the gospel of Christ. You must take the gospel as it is without any modification or qualification. So if you want blessedness, you must start with righteousness; otherwise you will never know it.

If you want blessedness, you must start with
righteousness.

Now we have here another example and illustration of that selfsame thing. "Let not your heart be troubled"—do you want a quiet heart? "Very well," says our Lord in effect to these men, "but I am not going to discuss with you a *direct* means of obtaining the quiet heart. If you want that, this is what you must do: 'Believe in God, believe also in me.'" Before we begin to consider our initial states and conditions, before we begin to consider our life in this world, the Bible invites us to consider our relationship to God. I think it is obvious why the world is as it is today. It is because men and women are all trying to obtain happiness directly. We are leaving out the fundamental principles, and we are doomed to experience failure and disappointment. We must start at the beginning. And *this* is the beginning. So we shall not discuss any further the means and methods to happiness and peace and joy; the cultures of man do that. The Bible says we should desire to have righteousness. It takes us right out of our narrowly confined, rather selfish interest and says, "Before you discuss together whether you are happy or not, we will start by discussing *you*, you in your relationship to God."

Let us, then, look at it like this: what does belief in God mean? This is one of those fundamental things that we tend to take for granted. We say, "I have always believed in God." The disciples believed in God in that way, and our Lord knew that perfectly well. But if those disciples had really been believing in God, they would not have been unhappy. To have a troubled heart means that you are not believing in God truly. There is something wrong in your belief; otherwise you would not be like that. There is nothing more fatal than to assume these things. "Of course I believe in God!" we say, but are we certain that we do?

If those disciples had really been believing in God,
they would not have been unhappy. To have a troubled
heart means that you are not believing in God truly.

An alternative way of asking that question is to put it the other way round. Is your heart at rest as you look at yourself and contemplate the state of the world? Is there peace in your soul as you look into the future and try to visualize yourself if certain things were to come to pass? We have considered these, the ills of life and all the various things that come and disturb our equanimity. So the vital question to ask is, do we have peace of heart? Are we ready to face all and to go through victoriously? That is what matters.

When we read Hebrews 11 and take a walk through that gallery of the heroes of faith, we see men and women who lived in this world, exactly as we do. Yet the amazing thing about them is that they lived their lives in an entirely different manner from other people. They triumphed; they had a joy and a peace and a happiness that all the things they had to endure could not disturb. Therefore, the way to approach this question is to discover their secret. What enabled them to do this? Well, the author of Hebrews gives a key to the answer in the sixth verse, where he puts it like this: "He that cometh to God must believe that he is, and that he is a rewarder of them that diligently seek him." That is just another way of saying what our Lord says here: "Let not your heart be troubled . . . believe in God."

So, then, what does that mean? Well, there in Hebrews we are reminded that the first thing at any rate is to "believe that he is"; we must believe in the existence of God. If you are uncertain of the being and existence of God, you will never have a quiet heart; it is impossible. I do not hesitate to make that dogmatic statement, for as I showed you earlier, the people who do not believe in God try to produce a kind of peace by not thinking at all. But that is not the solution. That is drugging yourself; that is hitting yourself on the head and knocking your brain out of action. While you are unconscious, you are not actively suffering and enduring pain, but refusing to think just evades the problem. The Bible challenges this way of thinking and says that without believing in God, the quiet heart is impossible. "There is no peace, saith my God, to the wicked" (Isaiah 57:21), and the wicked, ultimately, are those who do not truly believe in him.

We must believe that God is from eternity to eternity.
God is not a created being—God is.

So we believe that he is, and that means, first, that we must

34

believe that God is from eternity to eternity. God is not a created being—God *is*. Of course, we enter into a realm here that our minds cannot understand. We are entirely limited to the book that we call the Bible. There we have the revelation of this great being who tells us that there is no beginning to him. There is no start to God. He is life, he is everything, God the absolute and the eternal one, from everlasting to everlasting. You cannot prove the being of God; you just receive the revelation and accept it. If you could prove it, it would mean that your mind is of necessity bigger than God himself; so to believe in him is to believe in his eternity.

It is the same when it comes to believing in his might and power and his glory. God is almighty; he is all-powerful. His glory is such that no human being can approach him. He dwells in light; the glory of God is beyond thought and imagination. We must believe that about him, and we must believe in the so-called attributes of God—that he knows everything, that he is present everywhere, that nothing happens without his knowledge and apart from his sight. He is omniscient, omnipresent, almighty; and added to that we must believe that he is absolutely holy. Great terms are given in the Bible to describe this holiness. "God is light, and in him is no darkness at all" (1 John 1:5). He is "the Father of lights, with whom is no variableness, neither shadow of turning" (James 1:17). "For our God is a consuming fire" (Hebrews 12:29). Those are the terms that are given, and they are all just an expression of utter, absolute holiness, entirely apart from sin. He not only tempts no one with evil, but neither can he be tempted. He is in eternal brightness and perfection and beauty. We must believe that about God.

Then we must believe that he is the Maker of everything that is. He has brought everything into being. The cosmos has not just happened; it has not come out of nothing and from nowhere. God has set it upon its course. He is the originator and the artificer, the author and the Creator and indeed the sustainer of everything that is, whether animate or inanimate.

This is part, at any rate, of what the Bible means by believing in God. It means, therefore, that God controls everything. You see, if the secret of the quiet heart ultimately is to believe in God, then I must believe in addition that nothing happens apart from him. Yes, and beyond that, I must believe that he is able to do everything, that nothing is too hard for the Lord.

If the secret of the quiet heart ultimately is to believe in God, then I must believe in addition that nothing happens apart from him and that he is able to do everything, that nothing is too hard for the Lord.

Now you will find, as you read the Bible, that these have been very practical considerations for certain people. There was Abraham with that terrible dilemma over sacrificing Isaac. "What can I do about this?" he thought. "Is God able to do this?" And God said, "Yes!" And because of this, Abraham believed "that God was able to raise him [Isaac] up, even from the dead" (Hebrews 11:19). "With God nothing shall be impossible" (Luke 1:37), and what an essential part this is of the whole gospel of salvation and the quiet heart that it gives. That was the answer given by the angel to Mary when he went to her with the great announcement. She said in essence, "How can these things be? I am a virgin—I have not known a man sexually," and that was his response: "With God nothing shall be impossible." If you do not believe this, you will never truly have a quiet heart.

We may find ourselves in situations in which nothing and no one can help us except this God with whom all things are possible. This is the whole basis of belief in miracles. A person is dying; medical science has exhausted itself, has done everything it knows, with no result. But a body of simple people turn to God in prayer and faith and ask him to do the impossible, and it happens. Miracles are an essential part of this belief. So there are preliminary things that we must believe if we believe that God is.

But there are some other aspects of this matter as well. To believe in God also means to believe what he has said about life. It is all recorded in the Bible. I have already reminded you that the heroes of the faith were all facing this problem of life in the world, and that is one of the first ways in which the problem is bound to present itself to us. I face my problem, and I say, "What is going to happen in this world? What is going to happen to me?" And that raises another question in my mind: what is this world, what is this life of man, why are things as they are at this present time? I cannot have a quiet heart without facing these problems. I must have some explanation. My heart cannot be quiet, in a sense, until my mind is satisfied, and the Bible answers my mind and gives me satisfaction in telling me these things about God.

God has revealed certain things about life, and he has told us that he made the world perfect. "Through faith," said the writer of Hebrews, "we understand that the worlds were framed by the word of God" (11:3). It is by faith we believe and accept this, because he tells us so. And then, of course, we go on to believe what is told us, likewise, about the fall of man and of how sin came into the world. Alas, an element has entered into life. It is not part of the essential life; it is something fallen. A principle of evil has entered in, and that is the origin and explanation and source of all our ills and troubles. Now the Bible tells me that, and it is ultimately a part of my belief in God.

And then, of course, it goes on to tell me that in spite of all that, God, because he is love in addition to being light and holiness and righteousness, in his infinite mercy and pity has made a proclamation, an announcement, that he is going to do something about this world. He has said that he will operate in such a way in this world and life that out of the chaos he will again produce order.

It is still his world; he has not turned his back upon it.
He is not allowing it to sin itself into utter hopelessness;
he comes into it.

The promise was given right away at the beginning: the seed of the woman would bruise the serpent's head (Genesis 3:15). This world is not left to itself. So the essence of this biblical message, which gives us ultimately a quiet heart, is that this great God, whom I have been trying, inadequately, to describe, is intimately concerned about life in this world. It is still his world; he has not turned his back upon it. He is not allowing it to sin itself into utter hopelessness; he comes into it. So the whole message of the Bible is of God disturbing the course of life in this world and coming in as a Savior.

"Believe in God," says our Lord. But that, of course, involves a belief in something further. God has addressed mankind and set before us two ways, and he has told the world from the beginning that there are two possibilities confronting us all. There is the possibility of blessing, and the alternative is a curse. God has told us that whether we have blessing or curse depends solely upon whether our lives are lived in accordance with his way and plan or not, whether they are lived in obedience to him or whether they are not. "Live my way of life," says God, "and you will be blessed; if you do not, you will be cursed."

He said that, of course, to the children of Israel, and we have their example before us. These people had been involved in the captivity of Judah; they were God's people, but they were slaves in Egypt. And God, in a miraculous manner, went down into Egypt and brought them out. As their captors were pursuing them, he destroyed them in the Red Sea. He took the children of Israel into the Promised Land where he was going to give them wonderful things. But before he did so, he addressed them and said in effect, "I solemnly warn you that there are two possibilities before you—blessing and a curse. If you live in the way that I tell you," said God to those people, "then blessing I will bless you, but if you do not, then cursing I will curse you" (Deuteronomy 11:27–29).

These were God's own chosen people. But eventually, you remember, they lost their land and their temple and were thrown out among the nations—it is all prophesied in the book of Deuteronomy. And God still says that to everybody. The nation of Israel is nothing but a great example held up by God before the whole world. It is God showing us what he does to every being who is born into this life and world; it is either obedience or disobedience, it is blessing or a curse.

Now I say that God has a plan with regard to the whole world, a plan that he is working out slowly and yet surely. Things may *seem* to be taking their own course, and yet that is not the case according to the Bible. God is over all; he is manipulating everything. He allows a number of things to happen, but they are not outside his control. Go back to the Old Testament, and look at the nation of Israel. In the fullness of time God does what he says he is going to do. He allows things to go on until a certain fixed point. He knows the date for that, though nobody else knows; but a day is coming when he will bring an end to the history of this world. There will be an end of time, and he will finally judge the whole world and all its people, and then he will destroy all evil, and we will have "new heavens and a new earth, wherein dwelleth righteousness" (2 Peter 3:13). God will have fulfilled his old promise of restoring order out of chaos, giving universal blessing to those who belong to him. So the vital question for us is whether we realize that it is one or the other of these two. We must believe all that; it is part of believing in God.

But I do not stop at that point. I must go on to say this: to believe in God means that we must believe implicitly in the promises of God to those who do thus follow him and give themselves to him. I imagine that this was the thing that our Lord was concerned to impress upon the minds of those troubled disciples. "Let not your heart be troubled . . . believe in God." Why? Well, think of the promises that God has made to those who do believe in him. Read the Psalms, read the prophets, read God's gracious promises throughout the Bible. Our Lord had already reminded these disciples of some of them. He said to them, "Fear not them which kill the body, but are not able to kill the soul: but rather fear him which is able to destroy both soul and body in hell" (Matthew 10:28). "Do not be afraid of men," he said, "there is a limit to what they can do to you. But fear God."

"Let not your heart be troubled . . . believe in God."
Why? Well, think of the promises that God has made to
those who do believe in him.

He also said that nothing could happen to them apart from God. "Are not two sparrows sold for a farthing? and one of them shall not fall on the ground without your Father . . . ye are of more value than many sparrows" (Matthew 10:29, 31). "The very hairs of your head are all numbered," he told them (Matthew 10:30). You see, we are in a difficult world where things are happening to us and are upsetting our hearts. Since we are being troubled, what is the antidote? To believe in a God who has so loved me that he has counted the very hairs of my head. He is so concerned about me and my welfare that he knows me to that extent. When I really believe that this great Almighty God is as interested in me as that, then I know I have nothing to be afraid of, and my heart need not be troubled. "All things work together for good to them that love God" (Romans 8:28)—that is another promise. "*All* things," I do not care what they are. The promise is universal.

But, you say, what about war or illness or an accident or the death of a loved one—how can these things possibly work to my good? Well, I cannot answer that in detail, but I can tell you something that will include every eventuality and possibility. If you really believe in God, anything that may happen to you will drive you nearer to God, and anything that drives you nearer to him is a "good" thing for you. I will apply this to your experience as I apply it to my own; let us be frank and honest. When life is running smoothly and easily, and the sun is shining in the heavens, and everything is going well, how easy it is to forget all about God. We do not seem to need him, and we forget him, and we are far away from him. But then something goes wrong—there is an announcement of war, or there is trouble or an accident—and these things drive me back to my knees. I then get nearer to God, and "It is good for me that I have been afflicted" because "before I was afflicted I went astray" (Psalm 119:71, 67). Each one of us can echo the sentiment of the psalmist. God sometimes has to chastise us in order to draw us a little nearer to himself.

God sometimes has to chastise us in order to draw us a little nearer to himself.

D. L. Moody used to tell of the parents who came to him distressed because they had lost their only little child. They were unhappy and had a grudge against God. Their troubled question was, "How can you say all things work together for good?"

Moody answered them by telling them a story of a shepherd who was trying to drive two sheep across a river and was failing. They were running in every direction, and the shepherd could not get them across. Then he suddenly thought of a solution. He took hold of the little lamb of one of those sheep and carried the little lamb across the river, and the sheep immediately followed.

We are so foolish that God sometimes has to do things like that with us, and they are all done in love. You see, he took the little child, and that ultimately led to the conversion of that father and mother. The salvation of their souls was more important even than having a dearly beloved child for a few extra years in a passing world like this. "All things work together for good to them that love God."

But he has also said, "I will never leave thee, nor forsake thee" (Hebrews 13:5). That is another of his promises. "Believe in God," says Christ. Believe him when he speaks to you; believe what he says. Whatever happens to you, whatever may be your experience, he has promised he will never leave you. Underneath, always, are the everlasting arms. Therefore, says the author of Hebrews, in the light of all these things, "The Lord is my helper, and I will not fear what man shall do unto me" (13:6). He has a quiet heart, you see, because he knows that the Lord is his helper. "Believe in God" means believing in the promises of God.

He has promised he will never leave you.
Underneath, always, are the everlasting arms.

And the last thing it means is this: believing God thus, we are now ready to commit ourselves and our lives and our affairs into his almighty, loving arms. To believe in God is to be like those men and women in Hebrews 11. This was their secret. They so believed God that they risked everything upon that belief. They banked their all upon it, and they based their whole view of life upon it; they trusted him. There was Moses who forsook the courts of Egypt and all his privileged position. Why? Because "by faith . . . he endured, as seeing him who is invisible"; he had his eye on "the recompence of the reward" (Hebrews 11:27, 26). He believed God. Abraham had done the same thing long before. He came out of his ancestral home not knowing where he was going. Why did he do it? Because he believed God and had implicit faith and trust in him. And that has been the story and the experience of all the saints right down the running centuries. To believe God means an utter, implicit confidence in what he has said about himself and in what he has said about what he will do. It means casting yourself entirely upon that: "Let not your heart be troubled . . . believe in God."

To believe in God means an utter, implicit confidence in what he has said about himself and in what he has said about what he will do.

Yes, but there is still more! Jesus Christ also comes into the picture. "Believe in God, believe also in me," he says. There are difficulties about believing in God, and God knows that. So he sent his only begotten Son into this world to live as a man among men and women, and Jesus, looking at these disciples, said in effect, "You find that to believe in God is hard and difficult? Well, look at me again—believe in me also, trust me. If you trust me, you are trusting God; seeing me you are seeing the Father. 'I am the way, the truth, and the life: no man cometh unto the Father, but by me'" (John 14:6). There it is in its essence. He is the guarantee of everything that God has said.

Believe in God, believe in his Son, the Lord Jesus Christ, and commit yourself and your ways entirely to him.

3

BELIEVE ALSO IN ME

Then saith he to Thomas, Reach hither thy finger, and behold my hands . . . be not faithless, but believing. And Thomas answered and said unto him, My Lord and my God!

JOHN 20:27–28

We first of all glanced at the false ways of seeking a quiet heart because as I have already suggested, this is not only the great *need* of mankind, it is the *quest* of all of mankind. Everybody in the world, somehow or other, is looking for this peace. Some do it in a very rowdy manner, but still what they are looking for is a quiet heart. They indulge in shouting and in clamoring, and that is, of course, simply to try to silence and drown the voice of disturbance, and perhaps of anguish, that is speaking within them.

Thus it comes to pass often that appearances are most deceptive. People who look as if they are supremely happy and carefree are full of some great grief and carry a tragedy within them. We put on a bold face very often, and sometimes it is exceptionally bold because of the acuteness of the problem that is within. So it follows that anyone who is truly Christian will never take people merely as they appear to be but will feel a great sense of sorrow for men and women who are trying vainly to find a quiet heart by refusing to think. This includes all the people who plunge into a round of pleasure, who give themselves to the cults and commit intellectual suicide, who rush away for treatment to some psychologist or other, who drug themselves or take up certain ancient Eastern religions. All are simply trying somehow or other to find this peace that ever seems to elude them, this quiet heart that never seems to become an actuality.

But, of course, we do not stop at it negatively like that. We are concerned to give a positive exposition of what the Bible has to tell us about this vital and all-important subject, and I would remind you again that the Bible claims that it and it alone can really show us this quiet heart. I do not apologize for that. I state and assert it.

We cannot mix the gospel of Jesus Christ with
anything else; it is either this or nothing.
No compromise is possible.

We cannot mix the gospel of Jesus Christ with anything else; it is either this or nothing. No compromise, no coalition is possible. Unless we realize that we have to submit and surrender ourselves entirely to God's way, we shall never, as we have seen, experience the blessings that he wants to give us. Our Lord constantly said that very thing. He laid it down at the very beginning that this is the way to know his love and his blessing: "If any man will come after me, let him deny himself, and take up his cross, and follow me" (Matthew 16:24)—that is it. The two words "follow me" in a sense say it all; what you have to do is to forsake yourself and everything else and go after him. His claim is for a total allegiance.

Let us, then, continue to consider together the Bible's method of giving us a quiet heart. This, the Bible tells us, is an actual and practical possibility for us in this world of time. I have reminded you of those wonderful people of whom we are given a glimpse in Hebrews 11, men and women like ourselves who went through life with a peace and rest and quietness of heart that nothing could disturb. Furthermore, we are fortified in our consideration of all this by the long history and record of the Christian church. This is not theory; it is something that has been verified so often in the lives of men and women. I never tire of saying that there is nothing more exhilarating than to read the lives of God's people throughout the ages. Countless numbers of them join in testifying to this truth, which is the truth of God and which works in experience.

You can pick up the biographies of any of the men and women of God who have lived in this life, as you and I are living, who have known terrible troubles and trials but who have been able to testify that in the midst of it all, their hearts were perfectly quiet. The great stories of the saints and the martyrs and the confessors and, too, the great stories of many ordinary people in the church of God all testify to the same thing.

That is what I have to offer. It is my privilege to tell you that it is possible for you, whatever your position, whatever your circumstance and condition and problem, to be delivered from trouble and distress and pain of mind and of heart and to know the peace of God "which passeth all understanding" (Philippians 4:7). I want to put this before you as an actuality and as a possibility here and now.

> *It is possible for you, whatever your circumstance,*
> *to be delivered from trouble and distress and*
> *pain of mind and of heart and to know the peace of God*
> *"which passeth all understanding."*

So how is this to be obtained? We have seen that the great principle that we must lay down is that this is to be obtained indirectly and not directly, and the biblical method of doing this is not to consider our troubles but to start immediately with God. "Let not your heart be troubled"—why? "Believe in God." Immediately you are taken out of yourself, and you are confronting him. Half our troubles in this matter lie in the fact that the world is too much with us. We are in the midst of it, we are immersed by it all, and we are lost in the details. So what the Bible really does with us, in the first instance, is just to take hold of us and drag our attention away from the immediate scene to God. This is not escapism, because having brought us to confront God and his Son, it brings us back to the problem, and then it enables us to overcome it.

That is why the biblical method is such a healthy one. How different it is from many of the psychotherapeutic methods that, sometimes for years, delve into you and your experience and make you talk about yourself and bring up your past and so on. The Bible does not need to cite all the details of our past life; it recognizes that our fundamental need is God. So it begins to talk about him. That is where we must start. We have already considered together what was meant by that.

But now we must go forward a step. "Believe in God," yes, but "believe also in me," says Jesus Christ. Here again is something that is absolutely vital. So let me try to put it to you as a number of propositions. The first is that belief in the Lord Jesus Christ is the specific Christian message. Now I put it like that, briefly, because if we are not clear about that at the very onset, we will go wrong everywhere else. It is almost incredible, but it is still true to say that large numbers of people seem to think that being a Christian means believing in God in general. They say they are Christians, but when you ask them on what grounds, their answer is simply that they believe in God. Or they may say that they believe in a spiritual realm or in prayer, but they do not mention the Lord Jesus Christ—they have nothing to say about him. But that is not to be a Christian at all! Surely, by definition, to be a Christian means to believe something about this person, Jesus of Nazareth, the Lord Jesus Christ.

> *By definition, to be a Christian means to believe*
> *something about Jesus of Nazareth, the Lord Jesus Christ.*

The gospel of Jesus Christ, in other words, in its specific message, is something that brings us face-to-face with him. There is no sense or meaning in the term *Christian* apart from that. The Jew believes in God, and so does the Muslim, but they are not Christians because Jesus Christ has not entered their lives. The differentiating thing about the gospel is that it brings us immediately and directly into relationship with him, and what Jesus emphasized in John 14 is that we must believe in him just as we believe in God the Father. This is the particular point that makes Christianity Christianity.

Now notice, the gospel does not ask us to believe certain things about his teaching; it does not ask us to follow him in the matter of teaching. Rather, he says in essence, "As you believe in God, believe also in me. Put the same faith and trust in me as you do in God the Father. Believe in me as I exhort you to believe in him." In other words, this person Jesus is absolutely vital and essential to the Christian method of obtaining a quiet heart; and what I have to do, therefore, is to ask you to look with me once more at him.

> *This person Jesus is absolutely vital and essential to the*
> *Christian method of obtaining a quiet heart.*

Now our text is, after all, history; it is something that has happened. There was once a person on the face of this earth called Jesus of Nazareth, and here, looking at a body of men, he says in effect, "If you are going to have a quiet heart, if you are to enjoy peace and rest, if you are going to go through all that is coming to you with a quiet heart, undisturbed and even rejoicing, you must believe in me just as you believe in God the Father." And that is still the essence of the Christian message.

Do you have a quiet heart? Is it at rest at this moment, or are you troubled and disturbed? Are you worried, perhaps, about your past, something you did yesterday, last week, or last year? Is something troubling your conscience, making you restless and ill at ease? How do you feel with respect to the future? Is there something you know is going to happen in your life or experience or in your family that will make you unhappy? Are you face-to-face with some great change in your circumstances? Are you perhaps looking at the illness or the death of a dear one? Is there business trouble or worry? Is your own health troubling you? Is the future full of concern to you?

Perhaps you are disturbed about what you read in your newspaper and what you hear elsewhere as to the possible things that may be awaiting us—is there going to be another war, and if there is, how is it going to affect me? Is that your problem or trouble? I ask you, are you at rest and peace? Do you know what to do when these things come to meet you suddenly? Do you know how to find tranquillity and poise and balance and even joy in addition to rest and quiet? Have you found the secret?

Those are the questions. We have to face that this is the real problem of life and living. It is the one starting point in discussion about the Christian faith. As far as I am concerned, I am not going to discuss the Lord Jesus Christ with people until I have talked to them about themselves, and what I want to know about them is this: where do you stand at this moment? I must tell you that if you do not have a quiet heart, the real reason is that you do not know the person who says, "Believe also in me."

So then, let us look at him together. What does believing in him mean? What does he mean when he says this? Let me summarize it.

To believe in (or on) the Lord Jesus Christ is something that I can only discover as I read my New Testament. Someone may say, "What am I to believe about this person? I do want that quiet heart, but you say I must believe in him before I can obtain it. So what are you asking me to do?" I say that we must of necessity come to the New Testament for the answer to that question. I know nothing about the Lord Jesus Christ except what I find there. So many people say, "I believe this and that about him, and this is what I think." But they say that independent of the best source of information.

Let me emphasize that I not only go to the four Gospels in order to discover the truth about him; I also go to the book of the Acts of the Apostles. I also go to the epistles. Indeed, there is a sense in which I am prepared to say that I should go to Acts and the epistles before I go to the Gospels. I suggest to you that many people are confused about the person of the Lord Jesus Christ because they stop in the Gospels and never go out of them. You will never know him truly as long as you do that.

He said himself, as we find it recorded in the Gospels, that there were certain things he could not say to his followers and disciples while he was still with them. "I have yet many things to say unto you," he said, "but ye cannot bear them now" (John 16:12). You see, they could not understand his death until he had passed through it all. He said in essence, "It is all right. I will send the Holy Ghost, the Comforter, and he will explain all these things to you."

And let us never forget that the things recorded in the book of Acts had happened before these Gospels were ever written. Let us remember also that the first preachers of the Christian message did not preach out of the four Gospels; there were no such things. They went around preaching about Jesus Christ of Nazareth who, they said, was the Christ of God; and it was only later that the Gospels were written to those who believed and were incorporated into the churches.

Many people are confused about the person of the Lord Jesus Christ because they stop in the Gospels and never go out of them.

So if we want to know exactly what believing in him means, we must take the entire New Testament, the Acts and the epistles and the light they cast upon him as well as the detailed records we have concerning him in the four Gospels. And, of course, another advantage in doing it that way is that we find so many of the Gospel details confirmed in the stories of the disciples themselves; it was only afterward, in a sense, that they came really to understand. You remember how Peter at Caesarea Philippi made his great statement, "Thou art the Christ, the Son of the living God" (Matthew 16:16), and yet you know how he denied him afterward. But after he had seen the risen Lord and passed through Pentecost, what a difference there was, what a different outlook! And that is the same position from which you and I can look at the Lord Jesus Christ now, and thank God for it!

What, then, do we find? Here is one in this world of time who claims that he can give men and women a quiet heart. So the first question we ask is, who is he? If I am not right about the person who uttered these words, I cannot be right about anything concerning him, and I can never know what he has to give me. So we must start with him. And the answer that the entire New

Testament gives to that question is that he is none other than the eternal Son of God. Now obviously this is something staggering in its immensity, something that is really baffling to the ordinary human mind, but it is the assertion of the Scriptures, and we must of necessity start at this point.

Now the Gospels have their evidence with regard to that matter. They give us the account of his birth. They tell us that it was not an ordinary, natural birth, that he was born of a virgin, that he did not have a human father but was conceived by the Holy Spirit. Do not be foolish enough to try to understand that; you never will. That was a miracle, an act of God. But the assertion is that he was conceived of the Holy Spirit and born of the Virgin Mary. He was not a man like other men. He came into this world from eternity, in an entirely different manner. But nevertheless we are told that he really was born as a baby, that he was truly man though he is the eternal Son of God. We are also told that he grew "in wisdom and stature, and in favour with God and man" (Luke 2:52), that he lived life as a man here on earth, limiting himself deliberately in order to do so. The accounts of his birth are amazing. "But," you say, "the Gospel according to John does not give an account of his birth." John puts it like this: "In the beginning was the Word, and the Word was with God, and the Word was God" (1:1), and that eternal Word "was made flesh, and dwelt among us" (John 1:14). That is John's way of saying the same thing—the miracle of the Incarnation.

He really was born as a baby.
He was truly man though he is the eternal Son of God.

And then the New Testament goes on to provide us with evidence concerning his teaching and his claims. You get that in this very chapter that we are considering together. He did not hesitate to say, "I am the way, the truth, and the life: no man cometh unto the Father, but by me" (John 14:6). Thank God for those disciples and for their stumbling, blundering minds, their skepticism and their unbelief. I thank God for a man like Philip who said to our Lord in essence, "Look here, you are talking about the Father. Show us the Father, and it is enough for us." And Jesus looked at him and said, "Have I been so long time with you, and yet hast thou not known me, Philip? he that hath seen me hath seen the Father" (v. 9). We need to have this explained to remedy our unbelief.

Jesus did not hesitate to say, "Ye have heard that it was said by them of old time. . . . But *I* say unto you" (Matthew 5:27–28, emphasis added). And "I and my Father are one" (John 10:30). And "He that receiveth me receiveth him that sent me" (Matthew 10:40). And "Before Abraham was, I am" (John 8:58). Go through these Gospels for yourself; look at his words and teaching. Look at his claims. I have already reminded you that his claim calls for a total allegiance on the part of men and women. Here was one who did not hesitate to say to others, "Follow me. Leave everything; leave your father and your business, as it were, and come after me." He came to a man sitting at the tax collection booth and said to him, "Follow me" (Matthew 9:9)—and he did!

And then there are the recorded miracles. He makes use of that very argument in talking to doubting Thomas and doubting Philip. "Believe me," he says, "that I am in the Father, and the Father in me: or else believe me for the very works' sake" (John 14:11). "Look at what I am doing," he says in effect; "look at the evidence of the miracles!"

Do you want a quiet heart? Well, it involves a belief in
the miracles and in him who worked these miracles.

These miracles are recorded in the four Gospels because they tell us something about this person. They are facts; they have happened, and they are all part of the testimony and witness to him. Do you want a quiet heart? Well, it involves a belief in the miracles and in him who worked these miracles, and I challenge anyone who does not believe that, because you will never have a quiet heart without believing in him. And to believe in him includes believing in his miracles, these things that are attested and that proclaim him to be the Son of God.

But, of course, we do not stop at that, and this is where it is so vital to go on and look at his death and resurrection. Here is the astounding thing about it—here was one who made exalted claims but who was crucified in utter helplessness, and his dead body was put into a grave. "There is the end," said everybody, but on the morning of the third day, they found the grave empty, and he began to appear to his disciples and his chosen followers. They met together one night in a closed room for fear of the Jews, when suddenly, without the door opening, "Jesus himself stood in the midst of them" and said in effect, "Look at me," and he sat down and ate broiled fish and a honeycomb with them (Luke 24:36, 42–43). He was "declared," says the apostle Paul, "to be the Son of God with power, according to the spirit of holiness, by the resurrection from the dead" (Romans 1:4). It was that which finally convinced these men; it was that which finally proved that he was the Son of God, and that is why they went around, as recorded in the book of Acts, preaching "Jesus, and the resurrection" (17:18), the resurrection that proclaimed him to be the Son of God and therefore the Messiah and the Savior of the world.

Then there is his ascension and finally, as we read in Acts 2, his sending of the Holy Spirit upon the infant church at Jerusalem on the Day of Pentecost, a kind of postscript to it all. Furthermore, there is his appearance to Saul of Tarsus on the road to Damascus as "one born out of due time" (1 Corinthians 15:8), to give Saul (Paul) the evidence that made him an apostle and made him proclaim the Son of God as Savior of the world—Jesus, the Son of God.

Now that is the evidence that we have provided for us in the New Testament, and all the great arguments that you find in the various epistles show exactly the same thing. That is what it means to believe in Jesus—we believe all that about him. Or let me put it like this: I am asked to believe that into the very midst of the turmoil and the chaos and the unhappiness and the misery of this sinful world, the Son of God has come. Do you not see that this is the very essence of the gospel?

Do you want a quiet heart? Here is the way to have one—to believe that God has come to us in the person of his Son. We are not left to grope vainly in the dark.

Do you want a quiet heart? Here is the way to have one—to believe that God has come to us in the person of his Son. We are not left on the human level; we are not left to grope vainly in the dark. God has done something, and this is what he has done: he has "sent forth his Son, made of a woman, made under the law, to redeem them that were under the law" (Galatians 4:4–5), that he might give us a quiet heart.

That is the first thing, to believe the truth concerning him and his person. What is the second step? It is to consider *why* he came. That is the theme, in a sense, of this entire fourteenth chapter of John's Gospel, but I can perhaps summarize it for you here. He came to do certain things for us without which we cannot possibly have a quiet heart. He came to reveal God to us as the Father. Yes, the Old Testament saints did know something about God as Father, but not with the fullness that is possible to men and women who believe on the Lord Jesus Christ. They saw it "afar off" (Hebrews 11:13), but we can see it immediately and directly. Jesus has revealed the Father—"No man hath seen God at any time, the only begotten Son, which is in the bosom of the Father, he hath declared him" (John 1:18). That is John's message.

I will tell you what is even more wonderful. Jesus not only tells us things about God, he brings us to God, into a living relationship. He is the one who makes us children of God and therefore puts us into this particular relationship to God; and it is through him, and through him alone, that we obtain the gift of the Holy Spirit, which is vital to this question of obtaining a tranquil and quiet heart. It is he who really enables us to pray because he is our great high priest and representative. He goes on to deal with that in John 14. And finally, you remember, he offers us in this chapter his peace. "Peace," he says, "I leave with you, my peace I give unto you: not as the world giveth, give I unto you. Let not your heart be troubled, neither let it be afraid" (v. 27).

I can never be at peace truly until I am in right relationship to God, and the only one who can put me in that right relationship is the Lord Jesus Christ.

That is but a summary of the wonderful things that he has come into this world to do and to give to mankind. The key to it all, you see, is to start with the person of Jesus Christ and to be perfectly clear about him. I can never be at peace truly until I am in right relationship to God, and the only one who can put me in that right relationship is the Lord Jesus Christ. I will never get my sins dealt with apart from him. I can never be a child of God and a member of the family of God and expect God to work upon me and give me his own nature and his own life, and I cannot pray—I can do none of these things. But he gives me all of them, and thus he enables me to obtain a quiet heart.

I hope to show you later something of the work of the Lord Jesus Christ for us in our redemption and salvation. But we have been looking at the person himself, so let us close by looking still at him. This is what is offered to us in him. Here are we, on earth, in this difficult, modern world with all its problems, its trials, and its perplexities. We are conscious of weakness and of failure; we are conscious of the fact that the whole thing is too vast, too immense, for us. What can we do? "Believe in God," I say. "Well, yes," you say, "I want to believe in God, but he is so distant. He is great and almighty. He is so holy and eternal. What can I do to bridge the gap, to reach him?"

The answer of the author of the Epistle to the Hebrews is that in the presence of God we have a most sympathetic High Priest and representative, none other than this blessed person who looked into the face of his disciples and said, "Let not your heart be troubled . . . believe in God, believe also in me." Let us realize that, seated at the right hand of God in glory at this very moment, is one who has been in this world. He knows the sorrows of the human heart. He knows our weakness and our frailty. What a difference that makes to us! He knows all about us; so we can venture to come to him.

We are troubled in this life, says the author of Hebrews, but God gives us "grace to help in time of need" (4:16). When all things seem against us and threaten to drive us to despair, we do not know what to do, and we cry out, "How can we have this grace?" Here is the blessed answer: one seated at the right hand of God understands it all perfectly, and he "was in all points tempted like as we are, yet without sin" (Hebrews 4:15). He has been among us; he knows our situation exactly. Read the Gospels again; look at him. He never missed a case of suffering. He never passed by in a hurry when men and women were in anguish. The disciples tried to stop women from bringing their infants for him to bless them, but he said in effect, "It is all right; do not stop them. 'Suffer the little children to come unto me, and forbid them not'" (Mark 10:14). The poor blind man outside Jericho was crying out, "Jesus, thou Son of David, have mercy on me," and everyone tried to silence him, but our Lord was not in a hurry. He was going up to Jerusalem, but he "stood still." He called them to bring the man to him, and he healed him (Mark 10:46–52). He always had time to take the trouble to help others.

When he was dying and enduring that terrible agony upon the cross, even then he had time to speak to the thief dying at his side and to tell him not to be troubled because he would be with him that day in paradise (Luke 23:39–43). There was never such a tender, gentle heart. There was never one who had such compassion and an eye for the suffering of those who were off the trodden path. There was never one who came down so low, a friend of publicans and sinners.

He is still the same; he has not changed. John in his vision on the Isle of Patmos saw him in his glory, and yet he was still the same. He is still the same in your need, in your trouble, in your agony. When your heart is restless and when you are troubled and when you are disturbed, go to him. He said when he was here, "Him that cometh to me I will in no wise cast out" (John 6:37), and he is still the same. He will understand you, he will sympathize with you, he will give you all you need, and you will lose your trouble. He will give you his own peace, "which passeth all understanding" (Philippians 4:7). "Believe in God, believe also in me."

PART II

The Soul and Its Future

In my Father's house are many mansions: if it were not so,
I would have told you. I go to prepare a place for you.
And if I go and prepare a place for you, I will come again,
and receive you unto myself; that where I am,
there ye may be also.

JOHN 14 : 2 – 3

4

IN MY FATHER'S HOUSE

And I will dwell in the house of the LORD for ever.

PSALM 23:6

In our consideration of how we may obtain a quiet heart, we have seen that the first thing our Lord emphasizes is our relationship to God. When you face life, says the Bible everywhere, if you want to face it truly, you must, for the time being, turn your back on the problem and turn to God.

In other words, according to the Bible, you can only face life truly in the light of something else. The trouble with us is that with our limited perspective we let life overwhelm us, but the way to understand it is to step out of it and look down upon it. It seems to me comparable to aerial photographs. A good way of getting to understand and know a section of country is to look at an aerial photograph, or if you cannot do that, to climb a mountain and then look down upon the vast expanse. That is the way to grasp the whole thing; it is much better than walking along the road in the valley. You get the right angle and perspective. It is the whole view of life that is really tremendously important, as I hope to show you. Most people are defeated by life because they take a piecemeal view of it instead of looking at it as a whole.

So our Lord and Savior teaches us this at this point by saying first of all that you must start with God: "Believe in God." Not only must you believe certain things *about* God, you must believe *in* him. You must take him at his word; you must trust

63

him; you must have confidence in him. Hudson Taylor, the great founder of the China Inland Mission,[1] always insisted that the right translation of what we read in the KJV as "have faith in God" (Mark 11:22) really is, "hold on to the faithfulness of God." That is really believing in God; it is not a belief in your faith or belief itself, though that is important. Rather, hold on to the faithfulness of God. Have faith in him, be certain of him, for you will never master and conquer life in this world until, in spite of everything, you do hold on in that way.

Hold on to the faithfulness of God. That is really believing in God; it is not a belief in your faith or belief itself.

That is the great argument of Romans 8, where Paul, with his mighty logic, says you can be certain of God for this reason: "He that spared not his own Son, but delivered him up for us all"—who gave him to the death of the cross—"how shall he not with him also freely give us all things?" (v. 32). That is the certainty of God, and you must start with that.

Then, secondly, you must be absolutely certain about the Lord Jesus Christ and believe the vital truths concerning him. His whole argument here, as we shall see, depends upon those things; that is the very comfort he is administering. "If you do not believe me," says our Lord in effect, "and if you do not believe that I am going to do certain things for you, then I have no comfort to give you. But if you do believe, then you will have a quiet heart, and your hearts need not be troubled."

The next logical step is none other than obtaining a right view of life in this world. That is the order, steps 1, 2, and 3. We tend to start with the third step—we tackle the problem of life in the world. But consider the Christian way of approaching it: you do not rush at your problem; no, you step back. Picture yourself confronted by a great hurdle. You want to get over it to reach something else beyond it. Now ultimately the right way to get over that hurdle is to go back first. "But," says someone, "doesn't that seem foolish?" Yes, but that is what you must do—you go back, then you turn and run. And having worked up this momentum you clear the hurdle! And that is the biblical method everywhere. Do not go immediately to your problem; start further back.

Put it like this: if you are confronted by a problem of the unknown, a good rule is to start with the known; that is a favorite method in scientific research. Go from the known to the unknown. Do not start with the unknown immediately; start further back where you are sure of certain postulates. Lay them down. Then, having built up your case, go on to the inevitable result that must follow from it. That is exactly the method that our Lord is, in a sense, employing here. First view God, then the Lord Jesus Christ, *then* begin to approach your problem more directly as you come to your view of life in this world.

As we come to look at this, I am eager to put it to you in three main propositions. The first is that life in this world can only be viewed truly in the light of the next world. Jesus says, "Let not your heart be troubled: ye believe in God, believe also in me. In my Father's house are many mansions." You see how immediately, when considering the problem of life in this world, he goes to the next. That is characteristic of the biblical method. It is once more this question of perspective and angle and view, and therefore we have to follow it.

> *Life in this world can only be viewed truly in*
> *the light of the next world.*

Here we are in this difficult, troubled world of ours, wondering what is going to happen, hearing of rumors and alarms, wondering what is before us and how we will make it through. How are we going to live? How are we to face that? Well, Jesus says that, for a moment at any rate, we should look at the next world and then come back to this one. Now I know very well that when I say a thing like that I am saying something that is distasteful to the majority of modern people. "Ah," they say, "once more it is the old story of 'pie in the sky.' You Christian people are not realistic."

That is what has frequently been said during the last hundred years or so. This is the attitude of men and women toward Christianity; they say they are practical people, and what they want is something to help them live in this world. They are not interested in "pie in the sky"; they want some kind of practical life program from the gospel and the Christian church. We have heard a great deal of that.

Whether we like it or not, life itself has a way of forcing us all to consider what lies beyond it.

Of course, whether we like it or not, life itself has a way of forcing us all to consider what lies beyond it. Perhaps in earlier times life was so leisurely and complacent and quiet that men and women really regarded it as something almost permanent and everlasting. So all their energies and attention were directly to living life in this world, and if you talked about death and the life beyond, that was really unnecessary. But we, in our folly, have turned our backs upon God and the spiritual world, and we are trying to settle down in this earthly life. Suddenly came the world wars that destroyed everything, forcing us to think of the beyond. I cannot but think that such events have been a judgment that we have brought upon ourselves. We are beginning to see some point in considering the whole transitory nature of life in this world.

Now the Bible has always invited us to do that; it has always asked us to start in that way. So let me expound to you now what the Bible has to say about life in this world. It is temporary and transitory. It is nothing but a great journey; the world is something through which we are passing. We, according to the Bible, are but pilgrims and strangers in this world, sojourners. This is put in a classic phrase in the Epistle to the Hebrews: "Here have we no continuing city" (13:14). That is the message of the Bible from beginning to end. We are moving through; we are pilgrims and strangers, travelers.

But it also goes on to remind us of something else—life is also full of uncertainty and of accidents. The Bible always does that; it brings us face-to-face with the facts. The realism of the Bible in which I glory says that life is a kind of existence in which you never know what is going to happen next. Just when we are safest, things begin to happen. And the tragedy is that we have turned our backs upon the biblical view. You see, we really did believe that by political enactments, international relationships, and things like that we could make life in this world absolutely secure and certain. So we have our pension schemes and our plans for national health. I am not detracting from the value of such things. All I am saying is that we have been trying to persuade ourselves that we can make a certainty of life. But we cannot! Read this book of life, the Bible, and you will see that is one of its prominent messages.

Then, of course, its next step is to show that no security can be obtained, or is promised, in this life as such, and that to live for this life only and to rely upon it or anything in it is deliberately to court disappointment. Do you find this depressing? Well, if you do, all I have to say to you is that I am just accurately describing life, and to disregard facts is, surely, to be unintelligent.

If we are depending for happiness and joy and a
quiet heart, in a final sense, upon any individual
human being, upon our family, our home, our profession,
our money, our health and strength,
we are doomed to experience disappointment.

The Bible tells us that in this life and world there is no such thing as final security apart from the message of the gospel. So if we are relying for our final, ultimate happiness upon anybody or anything in this world alone, then we are certain to be disappointed. If our quietness of heart depends—oh, let me put it with almost brutal realism—if we are depending for happiness and joy and a quiet heart, in a final sense, upon any individual human being, upon our family, our home, our profession, our money, our health and strength, we are doomed to experience disappointment.

Every one of these things one day will be taken from us.

Yet is it not true that we, most of us, are building our philosophies upon such things? That is why the twentieth century was such an unhappy one, and the world wars shook everything. We have been relying upon life in this world; then suddenly comes a war and shatters it all. Now the Bible pleads with us not to do that because, as it tells us, these things are not going to last— "Here have we no continuing city" (Hebrews 13:14). We come, we go, things come to pass, everything is moving. "Change and decay in all around I see."[2] Everything is moving and is going to pass.

The Bible also tells us why all that is true. It is true because of sin. It was not meant to be like that, but that is exactly what sin has done. Sin makes us try to be independent of God. It sees to it that we turn our backs upon him and forget him, and as we think we are going to make life in this world last forever, we think we can do without him. But God comes in and says, "Thou shalt surely die" (Genesis 2:17) because of our sin. Then we are afraid! If only we could abolish death, then we would make a perfect world. But the fear of death is the thing that holds all of mankind in its thralldom, even as we try to ignore it.

The most important thing for us to concentrate on
is the life of the soul.

The next proposition is that because all that is true of life in this world, the most important thing for us to concentrate on is the life of the soul. We live in a world that is passing and transitory; it is a world of uncertainty. We never know what is going to happen. We never know when the end is coming. We cannot bank or rely upon anything. So what are we to do? "Well," says the Bible, "within you there is something that is bigger than life in this world. It is imperishable, and it is called the soul." That is something that goes on when the body dies and the world ends; it will go on "beyond the veil." Concentrate on that! The soul is what matters—not the external life, but this inner life.

Now our Lord himself, as we have seen, put that very clearly. He was sending his disciples out to preach. They were fearful and apprehensive, and he told them in summary, "Yes, it is quite possible that because you are preaching the gospel, men may actually kill you, but do not be afraid of them. 'Fear not them which kill the body, but are not able to kill the soul'" (Matthew 10:28). Enemies may destroy our body, but they cannot touch our soul. The soul is imperishable. It cannot be attacked; it is inviolable. Therefore, concentrate on the life of the soul.

Is that not the great principle taught in the Bible everywhere from beginning to end, that we must all take the long view? Do you remember our Lord's picture of the rich fool who had been so successful as a farmer that his barns had become too small for him? He said, "Soul, thou hast much goods laid up for many years; take thine ease." "All is well; look forward to a wonderful time of prosperity," he told himself. "But God said unto him, Thou fool, this night thy soul shall be required of thee" (Luke 12:19–20). It is the soul that matters.

The main function and purpose of life in this world
is to prepare us for the next one.

And that leads us to the last proposition with regard to life in this world as it is described in the Bible: the main function and purpose of life in this world is to prepare us for the next one. Now let us be clear about this. That does not mean escapism; it does not mean that you turn your back on this world or that you despise life here. It does not mean that you shut yourself up in a monastery or become a monk or a hermit, not at all! Notice what I said—the *main* function. There are many other functions. Oh, yes, carry on in business or in your profession or in your family life, live it to the maximum; but never forget that the main object of life in this world is to prepare us for the next. That is the whole philosophy of the Bible. It is the secret of all the saints; read again that eleventh chapter of Hebrews. The secret of every one of those men and women was that they were looking "for a city which hath foundations, whose builder and maker is God." They were "strangers and pilgrims on the earth" (vv. 10, 13), and they went on in the journey preparing for that which was to come.

That, then, is the first main proposition—that life in this world is only to be understood finally in the light of the next world.

My second proposition is that life in this world can only be truly lived and mastered, therefore, as we have a right view of that next world. We have seen that was the secret of all who have conquered and mastered life here. We have looked at it in our Lord himself. The author of the Epistle to the Hebrews helps us when he says, speaking of him, "who for the joy that was set before him endured the cross, despising the shame" (12:2). Look at the treatment that was meted out to him while here on earth. Look at the malevolence of his enemies, the bitterness of their persecution, the wrongs he suffered. Eventually there he was, being crucified, suffering agonies, and yet he went through it all more than triumphant. Why? "For the joy that was set before him."

That has always been true of all his followers. I ask you again to think of that mighty statement in Romans 8. "Ah yes," says Paul, "I am not promising you that you won't have troubles and difficulties—'We are accounted as sheep for the slaughter.' I am not going to tell you that you are going to have an easy time. I do not say, believe the gospel, then lie on a bed of roses for the rest of your time in this world. Not at all! Men may persecute you and try to destroy you, and hell may be let loose against you, but it does not matter."

> In all these things we are more than conquerors through him that loved us. For I am persuaded [certain], that neither death, nor life, nor angels, nor principalities, nor powers, nor things present, nor things to come, nor height, nor depth, nor any other creature, shall be able to separate us from the love of God, which is in Christ Jesus our Lord. (Romans 8:37–39)

That is it. Let the worst come! I endure it all because I am certain of what awaits me. I know I am being prepared for a life beyond this life. Indeed, that is the argument of the apostle Paul everywhere. In writing to the Philippians, he tells them that his own future is uncertain, he does not know whether he is to live or die, but he says it is immaterial to him. "For to me to live is Christ, and to die is gain," for it means "to be with Christ; which is far better" (1:21, 23). Read again the lives of some of God's saints throughout the centuries, and you will find that many of these people had to suffer many hardships, and yet what joy they had!

Do you remember that great hymn of Richard Baxter's (1615–1691)? If ever a man had trouble in this life, it was he. Yet he wrote:

> *Lord, it belongs not to my care*
> *Whether I die or live;*
> *To love and serve Thee is my share,*
> *And this Thy grace must give.*
>
> *If life be long, I will be glad,*
> *That I may long obey;*
> *If short, yet why should I be sad*
> *To welcome endless day?*

Do you sense that quiet calm? What is it based on? It is based on the certainty of where he is going. He knows what awaits him, and that is true of every saint who has lived in the world.

So let us face this quietness practically together. What of you? What of your view of that next world, your view of death, your view of the life that lies beyond death? Does it frighten you? Does it seem strange to you? Does thinking about it like this help you or does it depress you? What is your view of it? That is the greatest question you can ever face. We have to face it. We cannot avoid it. What is your feeling about it? Do you have this blessed certainty? Or does the thought of death and leaving this world and going on leave you with a sense of despair and fear and strangeness? That is the question. It all depends upon your view of the next world, and that, of course, depends ultimately upon your view of God and upon your view of the Lord Jesus Christ.

Do you have this blessed certainty?
Or does the thought of death leave you with
a sense of despair and fear and strangeness?

What our Lord said about it to these men was basically this: "I am going to die and leave you, and you too eventually will have to die. But do not be alarmed. Let not your heart be troubled. Why? Where does death lead to? It leads to my Father's house. You know," he said in effect, "I have never kept anything back from you. I have never withheld anything that is unpleasant. I have always spoken the truth. If it were true that you would never see me again, I would tell you, but it is not like that—I am telling you the truth about the next life."

What a specter, what a horrible thing death is to most of us. We regard it as a terrible monster that is going to grip us. Death, we say, is the most terrible thing of all, the thing to avoid. No, says Christ, death is nothing but the door of entry to my Father's house for his followers—"In my Father's house are many mansions."

We tend to think of ourselves after death, do we not, as in some disembodied state in some great eternity where all is strange and terrible. But it is really to go home, if you are a child of God, if you are a brother or sister of the Lord Jesus Christ. God is not some terrible awful power, away in some distant eternity; he is your Father. He is one who loves you with a love you cannot imagine. Thank God for human love, but, my dear friends, our human love pales into insignificance and nothingness by the side of the love of God toward those who belong to him. "My Father's house" is a glorious home.

But what else does it mean? It means to be with Christ. "I go," he said, "to prepare a place for you. And if I go and prepare a place for you, I will come again, and receive you unto myself; that where I am, ye may be also." Have you not sometimes felt, as you read the Gospels, that you would give the whole world and more if you could but spend an afternoon with him? It must have been marvelous to look into his eyes and into his face and to feel his glorious presence! But if you believe on him and trust him, from the moment you die you will spend the endless ages of eternity with him, in the presence of this blessed person, enjoying him, sharing his glorious life without end.

"In my Father's house are many mansions.
There is room enough for all of you."

I rather like this expression *mansions*—"In my Father's house are many mansions." "You need not be afraid. There is room enough for all of you," says Christ. A mansion—what does that suggest? Security, being surrounded by a permanent dwelling place. Here in this life I am in a tabernacle, in a tent; it is moving nightly, daily. But there I will enjoy security, stability, rest, a home fully furnished, everything prepared for me, peace and joy, everything I would like to be there awaiting me, everything my heart can desire supplied in all its fullness and beyond my imagination. "In my Father's house are many mansions." You and I can be absolutely certain of this "because," he says again, "if it were not so, I would have told you—believe me, trust yourself to me."

Now I think you will agree with me that this is the thing that matters. If I know for certain that awaits me, then I say let this world do its very worst to me—it can never touch that which abides. That is certain, that is absolute. Yes, though men may do their worst and hell may indeed be let loose, yet "there remaineth . . . a rest to the people of God" (Hebrews 4:9). "A city which hath foundations" (Hebrews 11:10) is above the flux of time. It is the home of God, and its glory can never be tarnished or diminished.

Do you believe that? That is the only comfort, finally, in a world like this, but the way to know it for certain as regards yourself is to believe God, to believe the Lord Jesus Christ. He has gone to prepare that place for you, and he will come again and receive you unto himself. Realize that your soul is the one thing that matters. I cannot guarantee anything about your body. Anything may happen; you may even be dead in a matter of days. But I can guarantee you about your soul. If you put your immortal soul into the safekeeping of the Son of God, it does not matter what may happen to you in this world, and in time when you come to the end of your life, he will be there with you, and he will take hold of you, and he will carry you through. He will open the door of the mansion he has prepared for you, and you will enter in and begin to enjoy what you will continue to enjoy through all eternity.

Realize that your soul is the one thing that matters.

So that, too, is the secret of the quiet heart. Always keep that first, and never forget it. However happy you may be, never forget that, because if your happiness depends upon the world or anything in it, it is bound to come to an end. Keep that first, and having kept that first, enjoy everything else to your heart's content. Realize, above everything else, that if you are truly Christ's, then nothing and no one will ever be able to separate you from him and from the love of God that is in him. Believe in God; believe in the Lord Jesus Christ as the Son of God, as the Savior of your soul. He has gone to prepare a place for you, and you can be certain of your eternal inheritance.

5

I GO TO PREPARE A PLACE FOR YOU

And I John saw the holy city, new Jerusalem, coming down
from God out of heaven, prepared as a bride adorned for
her husband. . . . God himself shall be with them, and be
their God. And God shall wipe away all tears from their
eyes; and there shall be no more death, neither sorrow, nor
crying, neither shall there be any more pain: for the former
things are passed away.

REVELATION 21:2–4

One of the most outstanding characteristics of the gospel of
Jesus Christ is its extraordinary logic. This utterly confutes
the idea that the gospel is some sort of sob stuff. If you want
logic, here it is: it starts by inviting you to face facts, not to ignore
them and put on a bold front and say, "All is well" when all
seems not to be well. It tells you to look at life at its worst. Then
it gives you these mighty propositions and says, "Work them
out." So here is the next logical step that follows on everything
we have been considering. It is a crucial step.

Someone may say, "It is all very well to say there is a mansion for me in heaven, but the question that faces me is, how am
I going to get there?" And here is the answer: "I go to prepare a
place for you. And if I go and prepare a place for you, I will come
again, and receive you unto myself; that where I am, there ye may
be also." Now this is, of course, one of those great crucial state-

ments of the gospel of our Lord Jesus Christ. Indeed let me add to that: it is one of the most wonderful things the blessed Son of God ever uttered. "I go to prepare a place for you"—the whole of the gospel is in that statement; in that one verse is packed the whole of Christian theology and doctrine.

> *"I go to prepare a place for you"—the whole of the gospel is in that statement.*

Now there is nothing more tragic, it seems to me, in the long history of the Christian church and her preaching of the gospel than the way in which this statement, of all statements, has been so frequently ignored and misunderstood. Its real truth and import are not often even considered at all because people take it sentimentally. Yet it is a statement that can only be understood theologically and doctrinally. We must stop to ask exactly what it means. It is a tragedy that men and women often do not do that. This is not surprising, of course, because this statement is the very central point of the gospel. It is one that Satan, the adversary of man's soul, has been particularly anxious to confuse and to confound. There has, therefore, been much trouble and dispute and debate over it.

Here, then, our Lord turned to these disciples and said, "I am going to die," and immediately they were troubled. Why? It was because they did not understand what his going and dying meant. I wonder whether we are any clearer about it. What is the meaning of the death of Jesus Christ? That is the question. What does it mean to you?

Many would say it is the greatest tragedy that the world has ever known, but they stop at that. They say it is nothing but the tragedy of a teacher who was misunderstood because he was ahead of his time. Some regard it as just the death of a martyr;

because of the enmity and jealousy of the Pharisees and scribes and the Jewish doctors of the Law, they say, he was condemned to death. The world was not good enough for him. His death was nothing but a great human tragedy, like that of Socrates. The world has always had its great martyrs, and Jesus of Nazareth happened to be one of them. Others say his death was nothing but that of a political agitator. Jesus, they say, had come to deliver his fellow countrymen from the Roman yoke, but the Roman authorities instigated a plot and did away with him.

All these explanations would have us believe that this is nothing but the death of a *man*, a martyr, a great teacher. Various other ideas have been put forward that more or less correspond to the ones I have mentioned, but we need not spend our time with them now. Let us rather look at the words as they are here expounded by our Lord himself. "I am going away," he says. "What am I going to do? I am going to prepare a mansion for you."

Do we in fact believe that the great goal that is confronting us is the goal of getting to the Father and getting to heaven?

Do we in fact believe that the great goal that is confronting us is the goal of getting to the Father and getting to heaven? That is the question that the gospel of Jesus Christ really does consider most; it is its one great central purpose. "But," says someone, "I want to know how I am to live in this world and how my world can be put in better order." Well, we may touch on that a little more in detail later, but I must report that there is no patent remedy in the New Testament gospel for bringing about world peace; it does not promise us that.

The one thing the gospel does promise us is eternal security in the matter of our ultimate destiny. It does not say, "Believe the gospel, and then you will never have any trouble in this life and world. If you only believe it, it can banish war." Not at all! It is an utter travesty of the gospel to believe that it does. Indeed men and women who believe that will be disillusioned, if they have not been disillusioned already. That kind of thing has been preached more in the last hundred years than it has ever been preached, and during that time we have had two major world wars. So the gospel's purpose is not to tell us how war can be avoided.

What it tells us is that whether there is another war or not, you and I are passing through this world of time. We have to die in any case, and the one thing that matters is how we can arrive at God and heaven and spend our eternity in the glory. That is what I am interested in, and that is the only thing that we should be interested in, because a day is coming when we will have no other interest and we will leave the world and everything else behind. Then we shall face that unknown eternity, and our great question—how can I know God?—will have already been resolved by that time. As John Newton wrote:

And may the music of Thy Name,
Refresh my soul in death.[3]

How will that happen? Well, our Lord is dealing here with that precise thing. He does not merely say, "In my Father's house are many mansions." He adds in essence, "I am here to tell you how you can get there." He makes a supremely logical proposition. It is something that he had to do for us, and, blessed be his name, it is something that he *has* done for us. He does not turn to those men and say, "Look here, listen to me, I will tell you how you can arrive at that mansion." He does not proceed to outline a program of what we have to do so that we may get to see God and spend eternity in his presence in heaven. No, what he says is simply, "I am going to prepare that place for you."

> *The gospel is not an account of how you and I*
> *are to save ourselves.*

Now this is the very beginning of the gospel of Jesus Christ; it is an announcement and a proclamation of what the Son of God himself has done for us. The gospel is not an account of how you and I are to save ourselves, how we are to climb the steep ascent of heaven, and how we can obtain admission for ourselves. It starts by telling us that we can never do it, but it goes on to tell us that he has come deliberately into this world to do it for us. The only one who can ever admit us into heaven is the Lord Jesus Christ, and what we have in these words is the beginning of his own exposition of the meaning of his death and resurrection and ascension.

"Now listen," he said to these men, "I am going to leave you. The time has come for the Son of Man to be glorified, and God is glorified in him." He was telling them that he was going to die, he was going to rise again from the grave, and he was going to ascend into heaven. His objective was to make it possible for us to come with him. Our entry into heaven, this entry into the eternal mansion and home with God, is something that is obtained for us by the Lord Jesus Christ, and by him alone. He has won our admission for us.

What, then, had he to do in order to make that possible? Well, let us put it like this. What did he have to overcome for us that we could not overcome ourselves? The objective that we have in mind is admission into heaven and into the presence of God. But certain things are standing between us and there.

Picture it, if you like, as a game of soccer. There is a man with the ball at his feet. He wants to get to the goal, but certain people are trying to stop him. He has to get through and beyond them. You and I are in exactly the same position. Or think of it in a military way. There is a city we want to enter, but certain people are standing in our way, fully armed, trying to prevent our gaining an entrance. How can we get through?

Now what our Lord said to these men is what he says to us, that he was going ahead in order to clear the way and prepare a place for us. What are the things he had to do? I simply want to tabulate them in order that we may see something of the meaning of his glorious death. There are certain things here on earth and certain things in heaven that had to be done before you and I could enter into the presence of God and enjoy the glory of eternity.

The first thing we encounter is the Law of God. God not only made men and women, he gave them his laws, through which he told them how they were to live. He told them that it was only as they kept those laws that they could come into his presence and have fellowship with him. Therefore, if we want to get to heaven, we are confronted by that legal demand. God says that unless we have honored and kept all the Law, there is no admission for us into the presence of God. What is in God's Law? The Ten Commandments are part of it; perhaps we need go no further to establish our need. I must worship God, and God alone; I must honor him and no other. I must not worship any idol—not only idols made of wood and stone, but also idols such as myself or my profession or my money or my loved ones or my home. I must honor God's Sabbath day. I must not steal. I must not commit adultery. All of these commandments are the Law of God. The Lord Jesus Christ summed it all up on one occasion when he said that this is the Law of God: "Thou shalt love the Lord thy God with all thy heart, and with all thy soul, and with all thy strength, and with all thy mind; and thy neighbor as thyself" (Luke 10:27).

God's Law demands of us, "Have you kept me? Have you honored me?" If we have not, we cannot come into the presence of God. We have to face that fact whether we like it or not. Ignorance of the law is no excuse, is it? If you break the law of your nation, you are arrested and taken into court. If you claim that you were not aware of the fact that there was such a law, do you think the authorities will release you? If you think you are going to get away with your illegal behavior, you are making a big mistake. The law must be honored!

Can we do it? I have never met a person who could, although many have tried. The other thing that confronts us is that because we have not kept and honored the Law, we are guilty before God, and we are under the condemnation of the Law because we have broken it. Is there anyone, I wonder, who does not feel guilty in the sight of God? Of course, we all meet foolish people who tell us, "I do not feel I am a sinner," but what they mean is that they have never committed certain sins. We are all sinners. To be a sinner means that you have not given God all the honor and glory that are his due. *All* the glory. Indeed, however good and however moral we may be, to be living a self-righteous life is the depth of sin. So we are confronted by our own guilt and the condemnation of the Law.

To be a sinner means that you have not given God all the honor and glory that are his due.

What else? Well, according to the Scripture the Law announces that the punishment of sin is death, and death is right there demanding his dues. He says that men and women are sinners, they have sinned against God. So he says, "I demand them," and he takes them unless, somehow or other, he can be dealt with. Death is a powerful enemy we have to face if we want to get to heaven. "The wages of sin is death" (Romans 6:23). That is why, as the author of the Epistle to the Hebrews puts it, we all of us, in a sense, spend our lifetime in the fear of death (Hebrews 2:15); we have a horrible feeling that death is going to take hold of us and keep us from God.

Then the last enemy that we have to face is the devil, because, again, it is the teaching of the Scripture that as the result of man's sin, he has put himself under the power of the devil. And it is the devil who wields the power of death, as we see in Hebrews 2:14. The devil is ready, as it were, to hurl us into death and into the grip of hell because we have come under his domination. He is there, standing in the pathway of anyone who tries, unaided, to arrive at God and to arrive in heaven at that mansion where one lives with God.

God is light, and in him is no darkness at all;
nothing impure or unworthy or sinful can enter into
his presence. So how can a man or woman enter heaven
without polluting it?

So there are these enemies and obstacles that we have to meet, whether we like it or not. We cannot avoid them; we have to face facts. But there is also an obstacle—I say this with reverence—even in heaven itself: God's own holiness and justice and righteousness. God is light, and in him is no darkness at all. He is absolutely pure, and nothing impure or unworthy or sinful can enter into his presence. So the problem is this: how can a man or woman enter heaven without polluting it? That is the problem that has to be met. How can God, in the words of Paul to the Romans, be just and yet a justifier of the ungodly (Romans

3:26)? And the ultimate problem is that even though somehow my sins were forgiven, how can I bear to stand in the presence of such a God?

Have you ever thought of that? We have all had the experience here on earth of being in the presence of some particularly good and saintly person. How unworthy that makes us feel; we feel uncomfortable in their presence because they are so good. Any special occasion, too, makes us feel nervous because of the greatness of the occasion. Multiply that by infinity, and then see yourself standing in the presence of God. The Bible tells us of certain people who had a vision of God. Isaiah, for instance, said, "I am a man of unclean lips" (Isaiah 6:5), while others hid themselves. The glory, the magnificence, and the holiness of God were such that they felt overwhelmed.

Have you ever thought of that? We will be taken into heaven and the presence of the eternal God. But first something must be done to us! Something must happen to us to hide the rags even of our "righteousness" so that we can stand unashamed in heaven and, beyond that, enjoy and look at God. People tell me they find it very difficult at times to enjoy reading their Bible; they find it boring. They find prayer, too, and prayer meetings and listening to sermons about our Lord Jesus Christ rather boring. If you are like that now, how do you think you can tolerate heaven? In heaven they do nothing but praise God and worship him and glorify him and magnify his name. They talk about nothing else. They do not talk of things that interest people here on earth; none of them are mentioned. So how are you going to enjoy heaven?

In heaven they do nothing but praise God and
worship him and glorify him and magnify his name.
How are you going to enjoy heaven?

Do you not see that something must happen to us? A lot of preparation is necessary before we can get to heaven. I thank God because he tells us, "I go to prepare a place for you." He has done it. He has answered every one of these demands. He has dealt with every enemy standing there sword in hand. He has dealt with every one of them, and the way is wide-open for us. He has lived the Law of God perfectly; he has satisfied its every demand. He has kept the Ten Commandments and the whole of the moral law; he has pleased God in every detail and is absolutely satisfactory in his eyes. And he has done it as our representative. So the first enemy has been conquered.

And then we come to our guilt and condemnation under the Law and, thank God, Christ has vanquished this also. He has taken upon himself the responsibility of our guilt and our failure and our utter condemnation by making himself an offering to God. He has presented himself as a sacrifice, and God has "laid on him the iniquity of us all" (Isaiah 53:6). Your guilt and mine has been transferred to him, and it has been dealt with—that second enemy has been conquered.

But then he goes on to meet the next enemy, for to meet the demands of the Law, you see, he inevitably had to meet death. As I have reminded you, "the wages of sin is death." The pronouncement of the Law was that anyone who failed to keep the Law should die, and he faced the demand of death. Death says, "I claim these people as the result of sin." So Christ had to meet death. He paid the required price.

Christ had to meet death. He paid the required price.

Death thought it had conquered him, for he died and was buried in a grave; death seemed to be victorious. But wait a minute! The morning of the third day arrived, and he burst asunder the bands of death and arose "triumphant o'er the grave." Thus Paul, addressing the church at Corinth, could say, "Death is swallowed up in victory. O death, where is thy sting? O grave, where is thy victory?" (1 Corinthians 15:54–55). Behold him, then, risen; the last enemy that shall be conquered is death, and it has been conquered.

But there I see still an enemy, this foul angelic being called the devil, who has consigned so many to death and to hell. He still waits and claims his power and tries to exercise his tyranny. He says to me, "Though you believe all that, I still accuse you." But again I have my answer for him: "Forasmuch then as the children are partakers of flesh and blood, he also himself likewise took part of the same; that through death he might destroy him that had the power of death, that is, the devil; and deliver them who through fear of death were all their lifetime subject to bondage" (Hebrews 2:14–15). He met the devil in single mortal combat many times here on earth, and he defeated him every time. The devil came to him during the forty days in the wilderness, and he defeated him there. He defeated him again in the garden of Gethsemane. Again he destroyed him on the cross when all hell was let loose against Jesus. He defeated and conquered the devil.

All these enemies that stood against us this side of heaven
have been met and defeated.

All these enemies, therefore, that stood against us this side of heaven have been met and defeated. Jesus has opened the way. So we are at the door and gateway of heaven, but, alas, we are faced with the justice and the righteousness and the holiness of God! But it is all right; he has even dealt with that. God himself "was in Christ, reconciling the world unto himself" (2 Corinthians 5:19), and the justice and the righteousness of God have been satisfied by Christ's reconciling sacrifice. Punishment of sin has been meted out on Jesus instead of on us. What man deserved has been cast upon Jesus. It is true that God can be just and the justifier of the ungodly at one and the same time.

A most amazing statement is made about this in the ninth chapter of Hebrews. "You remember," the writer says in effect, "that in the old dispensation, the earthly temple had to be purified with the blood of bulls and of goats. But, you know," he says, "that is not good enough for the heavenly tabernacle. The heavenly temple itself needs to be purified, and nothing but the blood of Christ can purify the heavenly things themselves" (9:18–28). What he means is that the blood of Christ is so efficacious that we can go into heaven without polluting it. His blood purifies it in that sense, and it also does it by reconciling the justice and the love, the righteousness and the mercy of God. So heaven is clear, and the way is open.

And then, of course, he does all this by giving us his own righteousness. So when we come to enter there, God will not see us as we are in ourselves. He will see us clothed with the righteousness of Jesus Christ. We are in Christ, and we are covered by him and his spotless, perfect life. We have everything we need. "I go to prepare a place for you." No one else could have done it, but blessed be his holy name, he has done it. Every obstacle has been removed, and the door of heaven is open for us.

Consider, finally, what it meant to him to do this for us. "I go," he says. Where is he going? He is going to the garden of Gethsemane to sweat drops of blood. Where is he going? He is going to be arrested, to be tried in court, to be mocked and jeered and laughed at. He is going to be spat upon, to have his holy body scourged. He is going to have a crown of thorns placed upon his head. They will take him and drive cruel nails into his blessed hands and feet. He is going to be nailed to a tree. Can you picture it happening to you, with nails being hammered through hands and feet? That is what he is going to. And, too, he is going to endure the mockery and the spitting and the jeering of the cruel mob; they did not know who he was or what he was doing. He is going to die and to be laid in a grave, he who is the eternal Son of God through whom the world was made and by whom all things consist. He is going deliberately to all that because that is the only way whereby the door and the gate of heaven can be opened for us. "I go to prepare a place in heaven with God, a mansion for you."

Beloved friend, have you realized that the Lord Jesus Christ has done all that for you? If you see it, if you believe it, you will agree with Paul when he says that you are not your own, you "are bought with a price," and therefore you must give yourself and your life to him (1 Corinthians 6:20). If you believe him, you can know for certain that he has prepared a place for you and will come again and receive you unto himself so that where he is, you shall be also.

6

I WILL COME AGAIN, AND RECEIVE YOU

Ye men of Galilee, why stand ye gazing up into heaven?
this same Jesus, which is taken up from you into
heaven, shall so come in like manner as ye have seen
him go into heaven.

ACTS 1:11

As we have seen, certain requirements have to be met before we can ever arrive in that mansion that is prepared for us in our Father's dwelling place, and we have considered how our Lord met them. We saw how he met and looked at the Law's demands, how he met the devil, how he met death and hell, and how he faced even the problem of the holiness of God himself. And in that amazing phrase of the author of the Epistle to the Hebrews, we saw how he even purified the heavenly places in order to ensure that our entrance does not introduce pollution there. So we are free to enjoy the blessings that await us in that mansion.

So we come now to the next step: "If I go and prepare a place for you, I will come again, and receive you unto myself; that where I am, there ye may be also" (John 14:3). Our Lord says in effect, "I will come back, and I will receive you unto myself. So you are not going to lose me; you are going to be with me throughout the countless ages of eternity."

Now it is generally agreed that this statement is a reference to what is commonly called the Second Coming of the Lord Jesus Christ. It may, in addition, have various other meanings about how our Lord comes to us spiritually and so on, and yet I think that obviously its main meaning is that of the Second Coming, one of the critical doctrines of the Christian faith, one of the great central doctrines of New Testament teaching and, therefore, a doctrine that of necessity we must consider together.

Let me introduce this subject to you like this: I am coming increasingly to the conclusion that one of the best ways of testing whether men and women are Christians or not, whether they really do believe and live by the Christian faith, is not so much to ask them directly for their view of the Lord Jesus Christ but rather to confront them with this particular doctrine. Instead of asking them, "What do you think of Christ?" or "What is your view of the person of Jesus of Nazareth as he is displayed in the New Testament Gospels?" I think a much more certain and subtle way of discovering whether people really are Christians is to ask them leading questions such as these: What is your view of what is happening in the world at the present time? How do you react to it? Are you surprised at it? Does the present state of the world and the prospects that seem to lie ahead of us fit into your philosophy of this life or do they not? Are you driven into the depths of despair by what is happening in the world today? Is this something that has come crashing into all your calculations and ideas, or is it something that fits naturally and inevitably into your view of life and of the whole course of history? What is your forecast of the future? What are you expecting of life? What are you anticipating in the realm of history?

People cannot answer those questions without telling you, plainly and surely, whether they are Christians in the New Testament sense of that term or not. There is no more direct way of discovering that than by bringing people immediately face-to-face with the world situation and asking them for their ultimate explanation. Alternatively, we can put it to them in terms of this extraordinary teaching of the New Testament with regard to the Second Coming of Christ.

In other words, does this doctrine of the Second Coming seem remote to you or irrelevant? Do you take the view that so many take? They say, "What I want from preachers is something that is going to help me live in this world here and now. You are talking about something that is going to happen sometime, about the reappearance of the Son of God into this world. If you were preaching like that many years ago, when life was complacent and leisurely and when it was an interesting thing to debate these theological points, I would not have objected. But, surely, with the world as it is today, you are not going to spend your time discussing these remote ideas?" Now if that is your position, you are displaying immediately your attitude toward the Christian gospel.

> *Does this doctrine of the Second Coming seem remote*
> *to you or irrelevant?*

Or let me put it like this: what is your view of Christianity and of its teaching? Is it that it is something that is to be applied to life, a great ethical and moral and social teaching that it is our business as men and women to apply to life and its circumstances? Do we believe that as the result of so doing we will improve the social conditions and the international situation, we will get rid of war and all sorts of trouble, and we will introduce the kingdom of God and make this world another paradise? Is that your view of it? Well, that has been the view of many people, and of all those in the world today who are astonished and unhappy, these people are the ones who are most surprised.

But one is constantly meeting large numbers of people who believe this argument. "I cannot possibly become a Christian," they say. And when we ask them what their problem is, they reply, "My difficulty is this—you claim that your message is one that has been given by God to mankind. Well, that gospel of yours has been preached now for nearly two thousand years. And for a time it had the monopoly of the thoughts and minds of men, but look at the state of the world! If the gospel of Jesus Christ is the thing that is going to put the world right, isn't it time it did so? So," they say, "I just cannot believe it." Now, there is only one thing to say to such people, and that is that they have an entirely erroneous view of what the gospel of Jesus Christ really is.

So I want to put my message to you in terms of that kind of question. I am looking at the sort of people who really are quite sincere, and I want to show that such a question is nothing but a sheer misunderstanding of the teaching of the gospel and what it promises. In their perplexity they regard the gospel as something that is to be applied to life, and by its application they think life can be reformed and improved. So it follows that they often feel that this teaching of the Second Coming of Christ is so remote as to be finally irrelevant.

What, then, does the gospel really teach?

Here in this passage I suggest we have it in a nutshell. Our Lord is addressing men who are continuing to live in this world. He tells them that they will have troubles and trials and tribulations. What comfort does he have to give them? Do you notice what he does? He talks about his death and the cross, and then he goes straight from his death and resurrection to the Second Coming. Not a word, for the moment, about anything in between. Haven't we noticed this before in the New Testament record?

We must be perfectly clear about what the gospel has to
say about the world and its history. It tells us that life
in this world has been vitiated and ruined by sin.

So let us divide this up. First, we must be perfectly clear about what the gospel really has to say about the world and its history. It tells us that life in this world and the whole history of the human race has gone radically wrong; it has been vitiated and ruined by sin.

Now that is, of course, as we must all agree, whatever our view may be, something that is quite fundamental. The whole teaching of the Bible, from beginning to end, is that the trouble with men and women, with life and with history, is radical. The real problem is sin. Sin does not merely affect the surface of life; it affects the very source. And the result of all this is that the life of this world is under the control of sin, under the control of Satan.

The Bible teaches, quite categorically, that sin is such
a radical problem that the world cannot now
and never will improve itself.

Some people today think that it is ignorant to believe in Satan. Well, if you feel like that, I just ask you to look at the world and at yourself and try to explain some of the things that happen, both within you and in the world, apart from the biblical teaching about Satan and the hosts and powers of evil, these malevolent influences that are unseen in the spiritual realm.

The next step in the argument is that the world, as it is in sin and under the control of Satan, cannot be improved. Indeed, I defy anyone to show that Scripture teaches that it can. The Bible teaches, quite categorically, that sin is such a radical problem that the world cannot now and never will improve itself; there is no hope for it in that way. So we begin to see why the man or woman who is truly Christian, who bases all opinions on scriptural teaching, is not a bit surprised at what is happening in the world today.

Our Lord and Savior himself said, "As it was in the days of Noah, so shall it be also in the days of the Son of man. . . . Likewise also as it was in the days of Lot . . ." (Luke 17:26, 28). He spans the centuries; he lays down the proposition that because of sin and the Fall, mankind *as mankind* is going to be no different at the end of history than what it was at the beginning. Therefore, nothing is such an utter travesty of the Christian gospel as the suggestion that because it is being preached, each generation will be better than the previous one, and the world will reform and improve, until everything that is evil and wrong will have been banished and ultimately all will be perfect.

The gospel never teaches that; it asserts the exact opposite. I do not apologize for saying that the Bible's view of history is profoundly pessimistic. Of course, that is why the Bible is not popular and has not been so during the last hundred years. Evolutionary theories and hypotheses are very optimistic; they all tell us that the world is going to be better and better and that mankind is evolving and advancing. Philosophers always want to be optimistic if they can be, and thus they paint this picture of improvement. And, of course, if you believe them, you cannot like the Bible because its realism contrasts sharply with these optimistic ideas.

It was Christ himself who said that there shall be "wars and rumours of wars" (Matthew 24:6). His teaching was that as long as lusts and passions and greed and jealousy and envy are in the human heart, wars will continue. You see, the Bible is not foolish enough to think you can have one thing on the personal level and another on the international level. As long as two people fight and quarrel, nations will do the same, and they are doing so in spite of all the fatal belief in the effect of education and international conferences to make men wise.

> *As long as two people fight and quarrel, nations will do the same, in spite of the effect of education and international conferences to make men wise.*

What is in the heart of man will express itself. We all know that the tendency in all people is to fight. The cause is sin, this terrible, malevolent power in the human race that drives us to self-destruction. The state of the world reflects the state of sin, which dominates our lives; this is the biblical message. Furthermore, the Bible goes on to tell us that as a result of all this, the world is under judgment, that the whole of human history is moving to a grand and ultimate climax, that God, because he is God and because he is what he is, has pronounced his judgment upon sin and evil and wrong. That judgment will finally be executed at the end.

So that is the first principle. The second is that the Bible not only says things like that about the world and human history; it also has something to tell us about God's redeeming purpose in history or what you may describe as a kind of divine history. The world is as it is because of man's disobedience and sin, but, thank God, he has not left it at that. There is a description of the state of the world in the Bible, as we have seen, but it does not stop at description. The whole point is to tell us what God has done about it.

> *The world is as it is because of man's disobedience and sin, but, thank God, he has not left it at that.*

What, then, is God's purpose? Again I start with the same negative. His plan and purpose is not to reform that world but to save people out of it. God's purpose is to take hold of individuals and to put them into another kingdom that is his kingdom and the kingdom of his dear Son. The very person who uttered these words that we are considering is none other than God's only begotten Son, the one whom God sent into this world to bring this gracious purpose to pass. When he was on earth he chose various ways to say to people, "The world is perishing; but come to me and become a member of my kingdom and you will be delivered, saved from the wrath of God." He has come, as Paul says to the Galatians, to "deliver us from this present evil world" (Galatians 1:4), to rescue us out of the dominion of Satan.

We have already touched on this in passing, but the effect of the gospel is to enable us to see the nature of life in this world and to bring us to see that what really matters for us is our soul, that our greatest concern should not even be the possibility of a third world war.

> *If I have not awakened to the fact that my soul and*
> *my relationship to God are infinitely more important*
> *than the possibility that my body may be destroyed by a*
> *nuclear bomb, then I have not started to be a Christian.*

Now I am not denouncing politics, nor international efforts to ensure peace. That is not my purpose. What I do maintain is that if I have not awakened to the fact that my soul and my relationship to God are infinitely more important than the possibility that my body may be destroyed by a nuclear bomb, then I have not started to be a Christian. I must realize that it is my soul, my eternal destiny, my relationship to God that matters. The effect of the gospel upon men and women is to bring them to see themselves as strangers in this world of time. They hang on loosely to time and the things that happen in this world and see themselves as pilgrims bound for eternity—that is the big, the thrilling thing.

The business of the gospel of Jesus Christ, therefore, is not to reform the individual or the whole world; it is to take hold of us one by one and to bring us out of it, to give us a new birth, a new life, a new beginning. It makes men and women children of God. It gives them a new outlook, a new power, and sets before them the blessed hope of life with God in eternity.

That, let me emphasize again, is the Christian message. The gospel is not merely an exposition of the Sermon on the Mount and its social application in order to make this world a better place. Men have been preaching that kind of thing for so many years and trying to put it into practice, but look at the results! To ask unregenerate people to live the Sermon on the Mount is mockery; they cannot do it. They cannot keep the Ten Commandments; they cannot even live up to their own moral standards. But how glibly people talk about "the social application of the gospel" and about bringing in the kingdom of God.

There is a kingdom of darkness and a kingdom of light,
and these two kingdoms are here together in this world.

Oh, the tragedy of it all! No, we need to be born again, to be regenerated, and the gospel offers to do that. So side by side in this world of time, you have these new people, the citizens of the kingdom of God, and those who belong to Satan. "Ye," said Christ to the Pharisees, "are of your father the devil, and the lusts of your father ye will do" (John 8:44). There is a kingdom of darkness and a kingdom of light, and these two kingdoms are here together in this world—that is another aspect of the gospel message.

The next principle is this: ultimately these two histories, these two kingdoms will meet, and then there will be an end. That is the essence of the doctrine of the Second Coming of Christ. This New Testament gospel tells us that as certainly as the Son of God came into this world as the babe of Bethlehem, as certainly as his disciples lived with him and saw him ascend into the heavens, so he will return again into this world, visibly, in a bodily form. You get this statement in every epistle. As Peter reminds us, the Lord himself said it (2 Peter 3:13), and the first apostles all preached it, but nobody believed it. The world has never believed this kind of message. But it is a part of Christian preaching to proclaim it.

Now I am not going to deal now with the various ramifications and theories and ideas about the details of this Second Coming of Christ. To me that is not the important matter. The important matter is to grasp this great central statement that he is coming again and that he is coming to judge. The world and its peoples, all who have ever lived, will be judged. There is to be a final assize. Everything that is evil and belongs to Satan and his kingdom will be destroyed; it will all be cast into the lake of destruction and fire. And, as Peter put it, there will be "new heavens and a new earth, wherein dwelleth righteousness" (2 Peter 3:13). Everything sinful and tarnishing will be purged out of the universe, and there will be a new world, in which there will be absolute righteousness.

And—you can be sure of this—all who belong to the Lord Jesus Christ, who have seen the all-importance of the soul, who have seen their dread condition under the condemnation of the Law, who have committed themselves to him, taking upon themselves the scorn and sarcasm of the world, those who have counted all things loss for his sake, who have denied themselves and have taken up their cross daily and followed him, those who have said, "I care not what happens to me as long as all is well between me and him"—these are they who will be with him in the new heaven and the new earth and will share and enjoy his glory forever and ever.

Those who have said, "I care not what happens to me
as long as all is well between me and him" will share and
enjoy his glory forever and ever.

"When is this Second Coming going to happen?" asks someone. And the answer is, I do not know, and nobody else knows. We are not to be concerned with times and seasons, but we should be tremendously concerned about the event. If you are Christians, said Peter to those early Christians, you will be looking for these things and hastening their coming (2 Peter 3:12). You will realize that this is the one thing that matters, and you will look forward to it. You will expect it; you will prepare yourself for it; you will realize what sort of a person you ought to be in the light of it.

People are so concerned to try to determine times and seasons. There are those who tell us that the Second Coming may be near. And there are people throughout the centuries, as Peter reminds us, who have scoffed at the idea and have said, "Where is the promise of his coming?" (2 Peter 3:4). This gospel has been preached for nearly two thousand years, they say today, but he hasn't come again yet. Yes, and they spoke like that before the Flood! People have always done that sort of thing, and when the Son of God came into the world the first time, it did not even recognize him. Remember, "One day is with the Lord as a thousand years, and a thousand years as one day" (2 Peter 3:8). I ask you again to face the facts. Look at the world situation, and try to explain it in any other terms than I have used. Do you not see that man, in his malevolence, his enmity against God, and his foolishness, is just fulfilling Scripture and its prophecies? And above all, I ask you to see yourself involved in all this.

Finally, what is the promise to the Christian in the light of all this? Let me remind you of it, and this is the thing that is most urgent for all of us. I do not want to be pessimistic; I do not know exactly what is going to happen in the world. But I do know that whatever may happen, each one of us has to die and leave this world. And what do I have to say about that? Well, death to Christian men and women, to those who have believed on the Lord Jesus Christ, means that they go to be with Christ. That is his promise to us. He said to that thief dying at his side on the cross, "Today shalt thou be with me in paradise" (Luke 23:43).

There are those who would say that one of the things that Jesus had in mind when he said, "I will come again, and receive you unto myself" was just that; that as you and I come to die, it will not be lonely, it will not be terrible, it will not mean going to some great unknown—he will be there. I am not sure that is straight from Scripture, but Jesus himself said about the poor beggar Lazarus that when he died, he was "carried by the angels into Abraham's bosom" (Luke 16:22). That is the death of a believer; it is not horrible. The angels of God will be there to receive you and to carry you to him. I am quoting the apostle Paul when I say that "to die is gain," for it means "to be with Christ; which is far better" (Philippians 1:21, 23).

As you and I come to die, it will not be lonely,
it will not be terrible, it will not mean going to some
great unknown—he will be there.

The Bible does not give us many details on this point. I do not suppose we could stand them if we were given them. The thing is too tremendous; it is too glorious for us to think of. But of this I am certain: when he comes again there will be a general resurrection. All shall rise; when he comes, followers of Jesus will "be changed . . . in a moment, in the twinkling of an eye" (1 Corinthians 15:51–52). There will be a great resurrection, and what our Lord tells us is that we shall be prepared for that new order, for that new earth, under those new heavens, even by receiving a changed body. This body of our humiliation will be changed. There will be no disease then because we shall not be stricken with illness and infirmities. We shall be "fashioned like unto his glorious body" (Philippians 3:21). We shall be like him; we shall see him; we shall be transmuted and glorified like him and will enjoy that bliss and those blessings with him forever and forever.

That is the comfort to those who believe on him. "Let not your heart be troubled." Do not feel all is lost because Jesus tells us, "I go to prepare a place for you. And if I go and prepare a place for you, I will come again, and receive you unto myself; that where I am, there ye may be also." I believe that I, miserable sinner such as I am, am nevertheless going to look into the blessed face of the Son of God and be like him and spend eternity in his holy, glorious, loving presence. This is true of any person who believes on the Lord Jesus Christ as the Son of God. If you believe that he died for your sins and rose again to justify you, if you give yourself to him and live for him, that will happen to you.

"Beloved, now are we the sons of God, and it doth not yet appear what we shall be: but we know that, when he shall appear, we shall be like him; for we shall see him as he is" (1 John 3:2). I suggest to you that in the midst of the darkness and the confusion and the uncertainty of this modern world, if you want rest, if you want peace, if you want quietness of heart, you will not find it by trusting in ideas on the reformation of this world, for these are all being falsified before your eyes. You will find peace only where you will find this assurance that whatever may happen to you in this world of time, nothing, *nothing*, shall be able to separate you from the love of God that is in Christ Jesus our Lord and the glory of being with him forever and ever.

Do you know this? Do you believe it? Give yourself no rest of peace until you have that blessed assurance.

PART III

No Other Way

I am the way, the truth, and the life:

no man cometh unto the Father, but by me.

If ye had known me, ye should have known my Father also:

and from henceforth ye know him, and have seen him. . . .

Verily, verily, I say unto you, he that believeth on me,

the works that I do shall he do also; and greater works

than these shall he do; because I go unto my Father.

JOHN 14:6–7, 12

7

I AM THE WAY, THE TRUTH, AND
THE LIFE

And because ye are sons, God hath sent forth the Spirit of
his Son into your hearts, crying, Abba, Father.

GALATIANS 4:6

I am the way, the truth, and the life: no man cometh unto the
Father, but by me" (John 14:6). In this verse we find again one
of those summaries of the central truth of the Christian gospel.
Of course, in many ways it is nothing but a summary of everything that our Lord had already been saying to the disciples,
but it became necessary for him to repeat it and to summarize
it all again because of the question put forward by the apostle
Thomas.

Now let me remind you once more of the setting. If we are
truly to understand and grasp this momentous statement, we
must bear that in mind. Here is our Lord about to go to his death
on the cross, and he informs his followers that he is about to
leave them, and naturally they become crestfallen and unhappy.
So he, recognizing this, administers to them this wonderful comfort: "Let not your heart be troubled: believe in God, believe also
in me." And then he outlines the great purpose that he is going to
fulfill by going to his death, to his resurrection, to his ascension,
and to everything that follows. "Do not be troubled," he says,
"do not be disturbed or unhappy. Do not regard my departure as

being the end of all things. It is not; it is far from that. In a sense it is only the beginning. 'I go to prepare a place for you.' That is why I am going, and I am going deliberately."

In other words, he confronts them with the great promise of the Christian gospel. It is his way of presenting to them the whole scheme and plan and way of salvation. "It is all right," he says. "I am going to leave you, and you will not see me with the naked eye. But I am going to the Father, and I am going to prepare a place for you to live with the Father. I am going to make ready for you that mansion that is awaiting you there, and when the time comes, I will come back and receive you and all others who believe on me unto myself, so that where I am, there you may be also."

We have been considering all that in detail. We have looked together at the purpose of Jesus' death on the cross, the whole purpose of the Resurrection, the Ascension, and what our Lord has even done for us in heaven. And then we have looked at that mighty statement about his coming back again, about the Second Coming of Christ, the final end of history, the consummation of the age, the final judgment, the destruction of sin and all that belongs to evil, and the ushering in of the glorious kingdom of God, the reign of Christ, and the glory of the saints.

So our Lord had been putting all that to these men, and he summed it all up by saying, "'Whither I go ye know'—"you have been with me now for nearly three years, and you are familiar with my teaching. Therefore, you know where I am going, and you know the way I am going. You know that the way ultimately will lead you to be with me in the glory." In effect, he turns to them and says, "Therefore, all you have to do now is to follow me. I have told you the plan, I have outlined to you the purpose. I have tried to make you see that I am going in order to prepare this glorious, wonderful prospect for you. So you are quite clear about it all—where I am going and the way to get there."

And then Thomas spoke, Thomas with his little faith. Thomas, who was perhaps still thinking in Jewish and materialistic terms about the kingdom, did not understand this. What was our Lord really saying? "Is he saying," thinks Thomas, "that he is just going to disappear for a little while and then he will come back fairly quickly in order to establish his kingdom among us? Is he coming back after a while to deliver us from Roman bondage and tyranny and set us free in a military and political sense? Is that it?"

"I do not understand this," Thomas said. "You say, 'Whither I go ye know, and the way ye know.' Well, I am sorry, but I do not know. Lord, we know not whither thou goest; and how can we know the way? The thing is a mystery to me. I do not know what you mean by going to prepare a place and so on and that you are coming again."

Thomas stumbled. And we should be very grateful to him
for his sterling honesty in expressing himself
so frankly and plainly.

Thomas stumbled. Probably he was blinded by his prejudices; so he spoke and made his double protest. And we should be very grateful to him for his sterling honesty in expressing himself so frankly and plainly. We have benefited from other glimpses of this man Thomas in the Gospels. They are all of a pattern. He was a plain man, rather a blunt man, and yet, to me at any rate, a very lovable man. He was a man whose heart, it seems, was, generally speaking, better than his mind. You remember that when our Lord was proposing to go to the house of Lazarus who was desperately ill, Thomas thought it was an awful mistake. He said, "Let us also go, that we may die with him" (John 11:16). That is the sort of man he was.

Even after the Resurrection, he could not quite follow it all. The death of our Lord upon the cross had been a shattering blow to Thomas in spite of all this preparation. Evidently Thomas had gone home, and the result was that when our Lord appeared in the upper room to the disciples, Thomas was not there. Though he was slow to understand, there was a ferment working in him, and he felt drawn back to the others. So he went back to them. But when they said to him, "We have seen the Lord," Thomas said in essence, "I won't believe it until I can put my finger into the print of the nails and thrust my hand into his side. I cannot believe it until I have actually seen him for myself." Then, you remember, our Lord came again and said, "Thomas, . . . reach hither thy hand, and thrust it into my side: and be not faithless, but believing." And Thomas fell at his feet and said, "My Lord and my God" (John 20:25–28).

So let us thank God for the honesty of Thomas because it was his question that led our Lord to make this momentous statement that we are considering. Thomas had a double difficulty, and our Lord dealt with it by making a double reply. "Lord," said Thomas, "we know not whither thou goest; and how can we know the way?"

"Very well," said Christ to him, "I am the way, the truth, and the life: no man cometh unto the Father"—that is the destination—"but by me."

Christ still speaks to us down the ages, and he says to us
in our troubled and unhappy modern world,
"Let not your heart be troubled."

Now all this is not only of interest to us in terms of Thomas and those first disciples, it is the most urgent and relevant question for us today. We are confronted by this great statement.

Christ still speaks to us down the ages, and he says to us in our troubled and unhappy modern world, "Let not your heart be troubled." That is the great pronouncement of the gospel; you need not be troubled if you will only believe this message.

But many of us are like this man Thomas. We say, "What is all this? We do not understand. What is it trying to say to us?" Well, the gospel comes right down to meet us. Thank God for the honesty of the Gospel writers also, that they did not hesitate to put in these human difficulties. John in his Gospel did not hesitate to report that Thomas was in difficulty and expressed his skepticism. So here our Lord amplified his statement and summarized, for Thomas and for us, the two vital and most essential points. And it is to these two great points I want to direct your attention now.

The first thing we must be clear about is the destination. What is the goal? What is it that mankind really needs in an ultimate sense? And this is our Lord's answer: our destination is God and the knowledge of God as Father. That is what we need; that is what we should be setting out for; that is our destiny. "We know not whither thou goest," says Thomas. "Well," says our Lord in reply, "I am going to the Father, and no man comes to the Father except by me. That is the destiny; that is the place to which I am going. I am going to the Father, and you must follow me to him; and what you must ultimately be concerned about is that you yourself should arrive there." Later he puts it still more clearly: "If ye had known me, ye should have known my Father also: and from henceforth ye know him, and have seen him" (John 14:7).

I can go on and point out to you that Philip, another apostle, by putting his question also at this point really emphasized and underlined the same thing. The moment our Lord said that, Philip said, "Lord, show us the Father, and it sufficeth us" (v. 8). And Jesus said to him, "Have I been so long time with you, and yet hast thou not known me, Philip? he that hath seen me hath seen the Father; and how sayest thou then, Show us the Father? Believest thou not that I am in the Father, and the Father in me?" (vv. 9–10).

There, then, is the first point that we must grasp and understand. Here we are, living in this world with all its difficulties and its trials, its pain and its contradictions, and we are like these men Thomas and Philip. We want to know where we are going, what we really need. And that is the answer. Our ultimate need and desire is the knowledge of God, and especially knowledge of God as Father. Philip, I think, puts it very well for us all—"Show us the Father, and it sufficeth us."

The greatest need of any person is to know God,
to arrive at God.

Now I want to unfold that statement a little. The greatest need of any person is to know God, to arrive at God. If we are not clear about that, we are not clear about the thing that you and I need if we want to know rest and peace and a quiet heart.

Knowing God does not mean only that we should believe certain things about God, nor merely that we should believe in the being and existence of God. I do not mean only that we should believe that he is the Creator, the maker and the sustainer of all things.

I can know God, not as someone who is far away
in the distance, of whom I am frightened,
but I can turn to him and trust him as my Father.

What the Bible, and especially the New Testament, offers us is an actual knowledge of God. We are to know him as our

Father. "No man," says Christ, "cometh unto the Father, but by me." So I can know God, not as someone who is far away in the distance, of whom I am frightened, a tyrannical someone who is set against me, but I can turn to him and trust him as my Father. "Ye have received the Spirit of adoption," says the apostle Paul, "whereby we cry, Abba, Father" (Romans 8:15). In other words, we realize that God loves us with an everlasting love, that he is so concerned about us that the very hairs of our head are all numbered, and that nothing can happen to us apart from God and outside his will.

This knowledge of God about which our Lord is here speaking means that we have fellowship with God. This same writer, the apostle John, in his first epistle (written when John was an old man), tells the Christians to whom he was writing that his great object was that their joy, even in this world of time, might be full (1:4). Indeed, the setting was similar to our Lord's many years before. He was leaving his disciples, and he wanted to give them comfort before he left. Now here is an elderly John, one of the apostles, writing to the Christians and saying in essence, "Before I go, I want to give you some joy and happiness even in a world like this. I want you to have 'fellowship with us: and truly our fellowship is with the Father, and with his Son Jesus Christ'" (1 John 1:3).

Now this is the central thing that is offered to us by the New Testament gospel. I can put it best of all at this point in the form of some questions: What exactly is your relationship to God? Can you say that you *know* God? Is he real to you? Is he personal to you? When you say your prayers, are you conscious that God is there and that he is listening to you? Do you have a filial affection with respect to God in your heart? Do you know for certain that you are in contact and in communion with him? When you turn to him in prayer about any question whatsoever, do you do so with confidence? Do you feel that the access is free and easy, that it is open and that you really are speaking to God in a personal sense?

If you say yes, then you know what I mean by fellowship with God. It is the very thing about which our Lord was speaking to these disciples before he left them. We can come to the Father even while we are in this world, having a certain knowledge of him and intimacy with him so that whatever may happen to us in this life, we are always in touch with God and always in communion and fellowship with him.

When illness comes or accident or war or trial or persecution or even death itself, I can immediately speak to God and know that I am in his hand.

In other words, we should be able to say, as the Bible says we should, "The Lord is my helper, and I will not fear what man shall do unto me" (Hebrews 13:6). So when illness comes or accident or war or trial or persecution or even death itself, I can immediately speak to God and know that I am in his hand. So whatever happens to me, I know "all things work together for good to them that love God" (Romans 8:28). Come to the Father—really come to know God, so that God becomes to you more real, in a sense, than anything you see. This is essential to obtaining a quiet and untroubled heart.

We must also know that we are to be with God at the end of the journey and in eternity. The *summum bonum* of all Christian living is to see God: "Blessed are the pure in heart: for they shall see God" (Matthew 5:8). We have been considering that. Let me emphasize again that the most important thing that we can ever know in this world is that a day is coming when we shall stand in the presence of God and share his glory forever and ever and spend eternity with him, knowing him, communing with him. We know and trust him now, while we go through this journey that we call life, and then at the end we will stand before him and hear him say, "Well done, good and faithful servant . . . enter thou into the joy of thy lord" (Matthew 25:23). That is the destination, and that is the great purpose.

So the answer to Thomas's statement about his not knowing where Jesus was going is that the Savior was going to the Father. And it is still the answer to every doubting Thomas. The Christian message is not about international relations or world peace. The central matter of the gospel is that we should know God and enjoy him for all eternity.

Of course, let me emphasize again that does not mean that we are indifferent to the world. I am not saying that because we are Christians we should not be concerned about the state of the world. But I do say that if we fix our attention only upon this world and this life, we are not taking the Christian view.

Christians start with the ultimate and eternal,
and then they come back to the present.

Christians start with the ultimate and eternal, and then they come back to the present. And those who have not prepared for the ultimate before they face the present are living in a fool's paradise. Whatever may happen in this world, this year or next year or any other year, if you know God as your Father, you need not be afraid of anything. Whatever happens you are safe, and your destiny is guaranteed if you are a child of God.

That, then, was Thomas's difficulty about the destination. Now let us look at his second difficulty, which was how to get to the destination. "Well," says Christ in essence, "the simple answer, Thomas, is this: I am the *way*." Now notice again that

Jesus does not merely talk or teach about the way or give instruction as to how Thomas may find it. His claim is, "I myself am the way." He does not even leave it at that. He goes on to say that he is the *only* way to the Father. "No man," he says, "cometh unto the Father, but by me" or "through me." Now this again is a momentous statement, and we must face it. Let me put it, therefore, as a blunt assertion. This Jesus of Nazareth, who here speaks these words, is absolutely essential and vital. There is no knowledge of God apart from him; there is no communion with God apart from him. He says categorically, ". . . but by me."

I emphasize this because I think nothing is more tragic than the way in which so many people still seem to fail to realize the absolute centrality and necessity of the Lord Jesus Christ. I recently read a book that purports to help men and women to try to find God and a quiet heart; but as I read it, I saw very clearly that Christ was not emphasized as essential. Yet here he is telling us himself that no man or woman can ever come to a knowledge of God as Father unless they come through him and by him.

Someone once described a marvelous experience of God that came to him as he listened to a performance of a Beethoven symphony. He said that as he listened to the entrancing music, he had this experience and he came to know God. Well, all I would say to that is that unless that experience led that man to see the absolute centrality of the Lord Jesus Christ, he is suffering from a delusion; he has had no experience of God. Unless this Christ, the Son of God, is in the central place as the *only way* to God, there is no gospel.

Let us be clear about this—there are counterfeit experiences. Certainly the man experienced something as he listened to the symphony concert. But the question is, was it an experience of God? Certainly people have felt a curious uplift of the spirit as they have seen a glorious sunset or as they have read some magnificent piece of poetry. You can read of strange and marvelous experiences that many people claim to have received. People will tell you that in your troubles and difficulties all you have to do is to sit down and begin to listen to God. You begin to speak to him, and you will have an experience. One man described how he had been living a careless and godless life, living for himself to make a name for himself, to make money, living for his family and so on. Then suddenly he came to see how wrong it all was, and he began to listen to God. So he wrote a book on his life and told how it was now being lived in relationship to God. And yet it is the literal fact that in that book the Lord Jesus Christ was not even mentioned once. If I understand this gospel at all, that man is not in relationship to God; he does not know God as Father.

> *I can think of nothing sadder than for men and women*
> *to think they are in relationship to God and then find,*
> *at the critical moment, that it has all been a delusion.*

We must be very plain and clear about this. The times are desperate, they are urgent, and I can think of nothing sadder than for men and women to think they are in relationship to God and then find, at the critical moment, that it has all been a delusion. There are counterfeit experiences; there is an enemy, the devil, who can, according to the apostle Paul, transform himself into a veritable "angel of light" (2 Corinthians 11:14). He will do anything, he will give any kind of experience as long as he can stand between you and this message of Christ. But here is the teaching of the Lord himself: "I myself am the way. No man comes unto the Father but by me." The apostle Peter, filled with the Holy Spirit, says, "there is none other name under heaven given among men, whereby we must be saved" (Acts 4:12). "For," says the apostle Paul, speaking of his time in Corinth, "I determined not

to know any thing among you, save Jesus Christ, and him crucified" (1 Corinthians 2:2). These men were Jews; they had always
believed in God. But what they had come to see was that there is
no knowledge of God as Father, no arriving in his presence and
spending eternity with him, except through this Christ of God.

This is the whole essence of the gospel. Jesus Christ is the only
begotten Son of God, and the message is that this eternal Son was
"made flesh, and dwelt among us" (John 1:14). He came as a
baby, and he dealt with the contradiction of sinners, and then he
went deliberately to the cross. He could have avoided it, but he
said that he must go through with it; otherwise he could not do
the work for which he had been sent. So he suffered the agony.
We see him sweating blood, and the nails were hammered into
his holy flesh, and he died and was buried in a grave. Then he
rose again. And I ask, why all that? There is only one answer, that
it was absolutely essential. It is meaningless otherwise. Would
God have allowed his only begotten Son to endure all that unless
it had been absolutely vital? It was the only way that the Father
could bring us to himself.

Whatever experience you may have, if something happens to
you in some mystical sense, whatever it may be, do not rest upon
it, do not rely upon it. I am prepared to grant that it may be an
agency used by God, but the test of whether it is or not is, does it
lead you to Christ? Does it bring you to see that his coming, his
living, his dying, his rising again is the thing that saves you?

That is what he says—"No man cometh unto the Father, but
by me." There is but "one mediator between God and men, the
man Christ Jesus" (1 Timothy 2:5). There is no other way, and
apart from him we are lost and undone; we need consider no one
else or look in any other direction. Do you desire to know God as
your Father? Do you want your prayer to be real? Do you really
want to feel that you are in his hands and that the everlasting

arms are around you in the moment of crisis and agony? Very
well, look nowhere except to Jesus, to this Christ of God.

All the knowledge that we can ever have is in him—
he is the truth.

And then he amplifies his statement and tells us that he is "the
way" in two vital respects. All the knowledge that we can ever
have is in him—he is "the truth." He does not merely talk about
the truth, he does not merely teach or preach—he himself *is* the
truth. The apostle Paul says that in him "are hid all the treasures of
wisdom and knowledge" (Colossians 2:3). "All right," says someone, "I agree with you that what I really need is to know God and
to know him as my Father, but how can I arrive at that knowledge
myself? Must I run to the philosophers or to the various books?
Must I hope that something mystical will happen to me?" Not at
all! Simply look at and come to the Lord Jesus Christ as you find
him in the Gospels, and then remember that he said, "He that hath
seen me hath seen the Father" (John 14:9).

O beloved friend, I know that the concept of God is baffling.
The mind boggles at the thought of him in his infinite greatness
and majesty, in all his eternity. So we say, "He is too far away."
And like Philip we say, "Show us the Father." But the question
has already been answered. If you want to know what God is
like, if you want to know his character, if you want to know
truth, look at the Lord Jesus Christ. Look at his love, his mercy,
his compassion, his kindness. Look at his readiness to help. He
never missed a case of suffering; he always had time to admin-
ister his blessing. "He that hath seen me hath seen the Father."
God is like that.

Do not think of God as an enemy, as a great potentate in the
distance, as some awful lawgiver. He is like Christ, and he wants

to be like that to you. All the knowledge you have about God is in Christ; you will never have any apart from him. Also, all you need to know about yourself you will find in Christ and in his teaching. He has shown us very plainly our desperate need. He has come "to seek and to save that which was lost" (Luke 19:10). All you need to know about your relationship to God you will find in him—*he* is the truth.

But let me emphasize this again, he is the truth and the knowledge of how we can be put right with God. You see, there is only one thing between us and God, and that is our sin. It is not our intellect that separates us from God. The barrier is sin, this barrier that has come in. That is the problem: God is there, and we are here. "Why do I not know him?" asks someone. Because of this barrier. The only way to have it removed is through the Lord Jesus Christ. He came in order to be my sin offering. "God was in Christ, reconciling the world unto himself . . . he hath made him to be sin for us, who knew no sin; that we might be made the righteousness of God in him" (2 Corinthians 5:19, 21). There it is—your sin has been laid upon him, it has been dealt with, it is cleared. Believe it, thank God for it, and you will know him as your Father. Christ "is made unto us wisdom, and righteousness, and sanctification, and redemption" (1 Corinthians 1:30). "Do you need wisdom?" says Paul in essence to the cultured Greeks. "If you do, go to Christ. He is the wisdom of God; all the necessary truth is in him." He is the truth.

But, thank God, he is also the way in this respect—
he is the life.

But, thank God, he is also the way in this respect—he is the *life*. Yes, I need truth and knowledge, but I also need life and power. Do you not know what it is to feel dead, to feel there is no spiritual life in you, to feel that God is far away? How am I to walk through this world? How am I to have communion with God when I feel so weak and frail? The answer is, he is not only the truth, he is also the life. Again, he does not merely talk about life—he gives it. "In him was life" (John 1:4). He has life in himself. All the fullness of the Godhead dwells in him bodily (Colossians 2:9), and any life you need he can give you.

He will quicken and awaken you out of death and sin. He will give you new birth, new life, and a new nature. He will come into you and dwell in you and strengthen you. As he said, "I am the vine, ye are the branches" (John 15:5). This means that the sap, the nutriment, the power, and the life are in Christ. He will spread it to you and express it through you, and the fruit will be seen in you, but the life is in him. "Without me," he said in summary, "you can do nothing, but in me all things are possible."

Do you feel your will is weak? Do you feel your energy is low? He will come to you; he will strengthen and energize your feeble will; he will enable you to resist temptation. He will take you above the obstacles and difficulties, he will empower you—that is what he has promised to do. He is life, and he will awaken you to life and a knowledge of God and fill you with his power. He will lead you along the journey so that, whatever your circumstances, you will be able to say with the apostle Paul, "I have learned, in whatsoever state I am, therewith to be content. I know both how to be abased, and I know how to abound. . . . I can do all things through Christ which strengtheneth me" (Philippians 4:11–13). A branch that is in the vine and experiencing the power of the living Christ is alive with life itself.

We need it all—spiritual life and strength and power and the ability to face all that may be awaiting us in this cruel world. It is all offered to us freely in Christ. And then, as we face death and the grave, he comes to us and says, "I am the resurrection, and the life" (John 11:25). He has conquered even death and the grave; Hades has been despoiled. And he energizes us, even through death and the grave, and raises us to immortality and incorruption. It is all in him. "I am the way, the truth, and the life: no man cometh unto the Father, but by me."

Call out to Christ immediately.
He will introduce you to the Father.

Are you in Christ? Are you relying upon him? Are you incorporated into him? Do you know God—do you know him as your Father? If you do not, then call out to Christ immediately. Look on him; believe on him; give yourself to him. Ask him to do this for you. He will introduce you to the Father. He is the only way whereby you can come to him.

8

GREATER WORKS THAN THESE SHALL HE DO

And the Lord added to the church daily such as should be saved.

ACTS 2:47

It is my intention at this point to do something that is perhaps rather different from my usual method. I propose to give you a general view of the message that is to be found in the Gospel of John, chapter 14, from verse 12 more or less to the end of the chapter. I do so deliberately and resolutely because I am anxious to call your attention to the kind of synopsis, given here by our Lord and Savior himself, of the results and the effects and the blessings that follow a true understanding of the meaning of his death upon the cross.

We have seen that our Lord, in encouraging his disciples not to be downcast, proceeded to instruct them. That is always his method of comforting. He never administers general comfort; his comfort is always based upon truth, upon doctrine. That is the essential difference between the method of the Christian gospel and that of all the cults and of psychology. They are all simply concerned to comfort; our Lord has a deeper and a greater object—to acquaint us with truth; comfort is incidental to that. No comfort should be trusted that is not based upon truth. The world is full of many offers of comfort. But we claim that this message alone is true and real and a lasting consolation because it is based upon the full truth.

No comfort should be trusted that is not based
upon truth.

We have been examining in detail the teaching that our Lord gave his disciples. We have just been considering how he dealt with Thomas's doubts, with the great answer, "I [myself] am the way, the truth, and the life: no man cometh unto the Father, but by me," and how he then had to go on elaborating this because Philip was in trouble also. "You talk about going to the Father," that apostle said in essence. "But if you could only show us the Father, or if somebody else could, it would be sufficient." And our Lord had to go over it once more. So he said, "He that hath seen me hath seen the Father; and how sayest thou then, Show us the Father? Believest thou not that I am in the Father, and the Father in me? the words that I speak unto you I speak not of myself: but the Father that dwelleth in me, he doeth the works" (John 14:9–10). "Do you not realize who I am, Philip?" he says in effect. "Well, if you do not believe what I am saying, believe me for the works—look at the miracles I have performed before you" (v. 11). To believe on the Lord Jesus Christ means a belief in his miracles. You cannot explain them psychologically. "Look at the works I have performed in your presence," he says. "Let them testify to you as to who I am and what I am."

That brings us to the end of verse 11. It is all about the person of the Lord Jesus Christ and his wonderful works. The miracles attest the person; the words spoken attest the person. Ah, but the most important work is the work he would perform upon the cross by dying, by being buried, by rising again, and by ascending—the great work of atonement.

If we are not agreed about those points, then what I am going to emphasize now will obviously have no meaning to anyone who is not in agreement. If we are not perfectly clear, I repeat—and this is the very essence of Christian preaching—that Jesus of Nazareth is none other than the only begotten, eternal Son of God, come down from heaven, incarnate, in the flesh, here on earth, born miraculously of the Virgin Mary, if we are not clear about these facts, there is no consolation for us in this message.

If we are not clear likewise about the meaning of his death upon the cross, all the rest is pointless because it is the very basis of everything. The great apostle Paul, as we have seen, in writing to the church at Corinth, says, "I determined not to know any thing among you, save Jesus Christ"—Jesus is the Christ, the Messiah of God—"and him crucified" (1 Corinthians 2:2). He set him forth; he placarded Jesus Christ crucified for the sins of men and risen again to justify them. That is the message. That is what our Lord has been saying in verses 1–11 of John 14.

But that was not enough for the disciples, and it is not enough for us. Something more is needed. He had been telling the disciples about their ultimate destination, and he told them that he was going to do this work and that he would come back at the end of the age and receive them unto himself. Yes, but they had to live in the meantime without his physical presence.

"We believe those things," the disciples thought, "but what is going to happen while we are in the world? We still have to go on living. What will happen to us between now and the moment when we die, or the day you come back to receive us finally unto yourself?" These are perfectly fair questions. Has the gospel nothing to offer men and women this side of their arrival in the mansion in the Father's house in heaven?

*What will happen to us between now and the
moment when we die?*

Our Lord answers that question by showing them certain
further profound results that would follow from his death and
rising again. He told them a remarkable thing at the end of the
chapter. He turned to these men and said that if they understood
these things, far from being sad, they would rejoice in his departure! "Ye have heard how I said unto you, I go away, and come
again unto you. If ye loved me, ye would rejoice, because I said, I
go unto the Father: for my Father is greater than I" (v. 28). It is as
if our Lord said to these men, "If you only understood what I am
telling you, you would rejoice because I am going. But you are
troubled because you have not grasped this clearly, you do not
understand." He went on to explain to them that his physical
presence with them was not the important thing at all. Indeed,
for the reasons I shall remind you of, his physical departure was
going to be a good thing for them. He said it again in the six-
teenth chapter: "It is expedient for you that I go away: for if I go
not away, the Comforter will not come unto you; but if I depart,
I will send him unto you" (v. 7). His departure was *expedient*,
a good thing, the best thing that could happen, as it were. "You
should rejoice," he said in summary.

*"It is expedient for you that I go away:
for if I go not away, the Comforter will not come
unto you; but if I depart, I will send him unto you."*

This is a double message. The first part is this: what is our
view of the death of Christ, its meaning and purpose? I wonder
whether we are not sometimes guilty, many of us, of exactly the
same thing as these disciples. Have we not often had the feeling

that somehow or another we have missed something because we have never seen the Lord Jesus Christ with our own eyes or have never seen him in the flesh? Have you not had that feeling, sometimes, that you wished you had been living in the days of the disciples? Have you not said to yourself, "If only I could have been with him physically, as Philip and Thomas were, I would not have found the matter so difficult. All would have been clear." We have the feeling that some of these men had an advantage over us, but it is terribly foolish to feel like that. It is a denial of our Lord's own teaching, not only in this paragraph but elsewhere in the Gospel records, and it is quite wrong.

Let me give you proof of that. This selfsame disciple, Thomas, after the Resurrection, you remember, refused to believe that the Lord had appeared to the others unless he could see Jesus for himself. And the Lord came again, and when Thomas saw him he made his great confession and said, "My Lord and my God." Yes, but you remember also what Christ said to him: "Thomas . . . blessed are they that have not seen, and yet have believed" (John 20:29). Physical seeing is not necessary. Indeed the apostle Paul puts it like this: "Yea, though we have known Christ after the flesh, yet now henceforth know we him no more" (2 Corinthians 5:16). So it would not help us to see him with the naked eye. The people who saw him in the flesh in that way, who considered him an ordinary man, were the people who said, "Away with him, away with him, crucify him." Even these disciples who received his teaching as they did stumbled. Let us get rid of that idea once and forever.

What are our views of his death? Do we regard it as a great tragedy? Are we like the disciples? Some people are troubled and disturbed and say, "What a stupid world to crucify this great Teacher! He wasn't old. He would probably have been able to go on for another thirty years giving his noble teaching. What a tragedy that he was cut off at that point!" Others feel that the result of his dying at that early age was that he just left us with his teaching and thank God for it! These troubled disciples felt somewhat like that.

Let me sum it all up by asking a question: do we realize what really eventuated from his going to that death? Do we realize the blessings that followed his departure? Do we realize that he went deliberately in order that these things might come to pass? Do we realize—let me put it with reverence—that the best thing that has ever happened in this world for us was that going of the Son of God to his death on Calvary's hill?

"I never understand why the church calls it
Good Friday—why not Bad Friday or Tragic Friday?"

I remember a man a few years ago asking me, "You know, I never understood why the church calls Good Friday *Good* Friday—why not *Bad* Friday or *Tragic* Friday? Surely, it is the worst thing that has happened in the history of mankind, and yet you call it Good Friday." That is a good way of addressing this question. Do you realize that Good Friday is *Good* Friday and that it is the best day the world has ever known? I am not referring to the men who cried, "Away with him" or to the men who put him to death, but I say that what happened on that day is the most wonderful thing that has ever happened—Good Friday, glorious Friday!

This is not a theoretical question, my friends; it is a very practical question. I have been pointing out, as we have considered this great chapter together, that its importance for us is that the greatest need of men and women in the world today is that of a quiet heart. We are troubled; our world is making us so. Daily we hear people telling us how serious things are. What everyone wants is a heart at rest in spite of what is happening around and about us, in spite of all these forebodings of evil. And here is the sovereign remedy, the only remedy. "Believe in me," Christ said. "Believe in what I am going to do. Take the right view of life as a pilgrimage to eternity. Believe that I am coming back to receive you unto myself. Believe this," he said, "and then whatever may happen, your eternity is safe."

"All right," you say, "but what about *now?* How do I manage today? What if I have to go through tribulation?" Here is the answer: he comes to meet us exactly where we are. He not only tells us about the ultimate—he prepares us for the present and the immediate future. Let me therefore draw out of this great chapter, from verse 12 onward, some of the results that followed his going to that death, resurrection, and ascension.

He not only tells us about the ultimate—he prepares us
for the present and the immediate future.

He tells us many things. The first is that his going does not mean that his work will stop but rather that it will increase. "Verily, verily, I say unto you, He that believeth on me, the works that I do shall he do also; and greater works than these shall he do; because I go unto my Father" (v. 12). What a marvelous statement! And it was relevant to the disciples. There they were, a group of men who had certain ideas about him. They said that he was wonderful, that his teaching was incomparable, that he was a perfect leader. They were looking forward to great days that were coming, when suddenly he said, "I am going away." And they said, "If he is going, that means an end to his work. If he is going out of the world, how can it be carried on?" And that was his answer—"greater works than these shall he do; because I go unto my Father."

Now he was not referring to physical miracles—no greater physical miracles were worked by the apostles than were worked by Christ himself. He was referring to something qualitative. What he meant was that he had referred to his physical miracles in attesting his own authority, but those who believed in him were going to do "greater things"—the spiritual miracles that followed Pentecost, recorded in the Acts of the Apostles and in the subsequent history of the Christian church. Have you ever thought of that? We tend to misunderstand the death of Christ at this point, and the misunderstanding is always due to the same reason, that we are somehow not clear about his person or his death. You see, if we think of him only as a man, as the disciples did at that point, we will not understand it. If we are only interested in his teaching, we will not understand it. But the moment we begin to understand the meaning of his death, the whole situation becomes entirely changed.

Let me put it like this. An incident is recorded in John 12 about certain Greeks who came, desiring to have an interview with Jesus. The message was passed on to him, but he did not see them, and in that connection he made this momentous and profound statement: "I, if I be lifted up from the earth, will draw all men unto me" (v. 32). In a sense, while he was still here on earth as a human teacher, he was only the Jewish Messiah, and misunderstood at that. "I cannot see the Greeks now," he said in effect, "there is no point in it. But when I die, I will become the Savior of the world, the Savior of mankind."

While he was still here on earth as a human teacher, he was only the Jewish Messiah, and misunderstood at that. "But when I die, I will become the Savior of mankind."

And that, in a way, is the very thing he was saying here. I

again say, with reverence and caution, that his real work of saving mankind happened after the cross. He talked about this, but the disciples did not understand it. He constantly told them about his death and resurrection, but they did not grasp it all. It was only afterward, as they looked back from Pentecost, when they were filled with the Holy Spirit, that they saw it. On Calvary's hill the fountain for sin and uncleanness was opened. It was by bearing the sins of mankind in his body on the tree that he became the Savior of the world. The work had to be done first, and then it could be released. If you like, it is there that the great source was tapped and opened, and from there the stream poured forth and made fruitful the whole world of men and women.

History confirms this. Take the accounts of the Gospels. Here was this incomparable preacher, this wonderful teacher, this miracle-worker, and yet he attracted only a few followers to himself. He was rejected and forsaken even by his own intimate circle of followers, and he went to a violent death upon the cross, which made the scoffers say he was a failure. And then you see a man like Simon Peter—the impulsive, unreliable Peter, preaching one sermon at Jerusalem, and three thousand people were converted and saved. Oh, yes, "greater works than these shall he do; because I go unto my Father."

The cross had to happen first. That was the essential preliminary, the matter without which there would be no salvation. It had to be done first, and then the power of the Holy Spirit came to apply it. Jesus' going away did not mean the end of the work; it meant the continuing and the carrying on of the work in a still greater and in a still more wonderful manner. I see new believers crowding into the kingdom on the Day of Pentecost, three thousand of them. Then I see Peter, called to the Gentiles at Caesarea, and the doorway to the Gentiles is opened, and I see them streaming in. And the gospel is preached throughout the whole world—"greater works than these shall he do." It is the death of Christ upon the cross that really gives to us and brings to us these great and glorious and wondrous blessings from God.

The second point is his help in prayer. "Whatsoever ye shall ask in my name, that will I do, that the Father may be glorified in the Son. If ye shall ask any thing in my name, I will do it" (John 14:13–14). What a long time we could spend on these verses! But I will summarize them. Here are these men, crestfallen, and they say, "In times of trouble we always turn to him, and now he is going away. What can we do? He makes the decisions, and now we will not have him to rely on." And his reply is, "Foolish men—you can pray to me. I will be there with the Father. I will be the great High Priest to whom your prayers will come. I will be with you in these matters, and when you pray in my name I will do it."

This message is relevant to us at this present time. If you are clear about him, about his person and work and what he has done, if you know your sins are forgiven, if you know you are a Christian, a child of God, then I say to you that he tells you here to go to him, whatever your need. Whatever your position, go to him in confidence, and he will be with you, he will be there. "Speak to me," he says in essence. "I am here, and I will present your petition to the Father." What a wonderful promise to men and women who may have to face things too terrible even to imagine. Are you preparing for things like that? Cannot you see that a time may come in your life when you will be so desperate that nobody will be able to help you and you will be left alone? What can you do? Child of God, speak to him; he is there. Christ tells us that he is going away in order that such a confidence may be possible. He has died for you; he has made you a child of God, and you can have the confidence of a child. You can go to God, knowing he is your

Father, and pray in the name of Christ. He promises to deal with your petition. I cannot imagine anything more glorious or wonderful than that.

He has made you a child of God, and
you can have the confidence of a child.

The next thing he told them is that his departure did not even mean that his work in them and for them would come to an end because he gave them the great promise of the Holy Spirit. "I will pray the Father, and he shall give you another Comforter [another Advocate], that he may abide with you for ever; even the Spirit of truth; whom the world cannot receive, because it seeth him not, neither knoweth him; but ye know him; for he dwelleth with you, and shall be in you" (vv. 16–17). This again is amazing and astounding. Do you see what it means? These men turned to one another and in effect said, "Well now, if he is going to leave us, we will have nobody to teach us. We have had all this wonderful teaching for three years, but, alas, it is suddenly coming to an end. We cannot remember all that he said, and we cannot go on. What will happen to us?"

"Silence," says Christ in effect. "I am going to send the Holy Spirit to you, and he will not only be with you, he will be in you. You know," he said to them, "this is going to be a good thing for you. I am a teacher outside you, but I will send a teacher who will be inside you. He will recall to you everything that I have ever said. He will lead you into further truth and explain it to you. You will have within you a source of knowledge that will amaze and astound you." That is why he said that it was expedient for them that he should go away. The Holy Spirit enters into the believer, and he has a teacher within him; he is given understanding.

The Holy Spirit enters into the believer, and he has a
teacher within him; he is given understanding.

This was the great theme of the apostle Paul. He, of all men, with his gigantic mind and intellect, said in 1 Corinthians 2, in summary, "The wise men of the world cannot understand this preaching of the cross and of the blood. It is folly to them." Of course, that is because they are trying with their natural, finite minds to understand, and no man can do it. But "the Spirit searcheth all things, yea, the deep things of God." The Spirit we have received is "not the spirit of the world, but the spirit which is of God; that we might know the things that are freely given to us of God" (vv. 10, 12). Look at these stumbling disciples, uncertain of the person, stumbling at the fact of his death, not understanding the Resurrection—oh, what hopeless men they are, and how dejected! Then look at them in the Acts of the Apostles, expounding the Scriptures, understanding Jesus Christ, understanding the meaning of his death and the atonement; preaching, writing, teaching, filled with a new understanding. It is because of the unction and anointing of the Holy Spirit; Jesus promised it, and it happened.

Admit your bankruptcy and failure. Ask him for the
unction of the Holy Spirit, and you will have it.

If you do not understand these things, you have but to take him at his word and believe on him and ask him for the Holy Spirit, and he will give him to you. Admit your bankruptcy and failure. Ask him for the unction of the Holy Spirit, and you will have it, and you will begin to understand and to know the things that have baffled you hitherto. What a wonderful promise! He will enable you to understand the course of history. You will no longer be surprised at the world or by wars and rumors of wars. You will see the unfolding of God's plan for the ages; with the unction and anointing of the Holy Spirit you will see the end. Do you understand? Are you running from teacher to teacher and from book to book? Here is everything you need, but you need the presence of the Holy Spirit within you to understand it.

And lastly, he said that his going away would actually mean that he would be with them in a more real sense than he had ever been before. "I will not leave you comfortless"—that is, "I will not leave you orphans"—"I will come to you. Yet a little while, and the world seeth me no more; but ye see me: because I live, ye shall live also" (vv. 18–19). And then come the sublime and astounding words that follow, when he said that he himself, and the Father too, would come and dwell and take up their abode within the life of believers (v. 23). "If you really understood these things," said Christ in essence, "you would rejoice when I say I am going away. Why? For this reason—I am going physically and in the body, but that just means that I will come back and live within you, not only by your side. I am going to dwell *in* you."

Amazing doctrine, baffling to the understanding, and yet true. "I live," says Paul, "yet not I, but Christ liveth in me" (Galatians 2:20). Christ says, "Behold, I stand at the door, and knock"—"I want to come in"—"If any man hear my voice, and open the door, I will come in to him, and will sup with him, and he with me" (Revelation 3:20). "Oh, do not be troubled by my announcement of my departure," he said to the disciples who were not clear about these things. "It does not mean I am going from you. I am coming back and will live within you." This is the supreme offer, the supreme blessing of the Christian gospel, that it tells us that if we but believe these things and commit ourselves to them, God will come and dwell within us, Christ will take up his abode in our hearts. So whatever may happen to us, whatever the world may do to us, whatever may be taken from us, whatever calamity may overwhelm us, he will always remain. He says he will abide in us forever and ever. In the flesh he came and he went, but now he comes spiritually and dwells within us.

In the flesh he came and he went, but now he comes
spiritually and dwells within us.

Now, I do not know how you feel, but as I finished reading and studying this chapter of John's Gospel, I said to myself that from now on I will pray the prayer that the great and saintly Hudson Taylor[4] prayed every day of his life. When Hudson Taylor died, they found in his Bible a kind of bookmark, just a sheet of paper. As he read his Bible, he moved the paper every day. On it was a prayer, and it seems to me to be the most vital thing we can ever pray:

Lord Jesus make Thyself to me,
A living bright reality,
More present to faith's vision keen
Than any outward object seen;
More near, more intimately nigh
Than e'en the sweetest earthly tie.

If only we know for certain that the Christ of God is in us, if only we can say with Paul, "Christ liveth in me," then we will be able to say with Paul that nothing that may happen to us can in any way "separate us from the love of God, which is in Christ Jesus our Lord" (Romans 8:39). We not only believe things about him, we not only believe on him, we are to *know* him and to experience him and his eternal, wondrous life being lived out in us. It is wrong, it is unscriptural, it is even sinful to stop at anything less than that. He not only died that we might be forgiven—he died in order that he might come and live in us.

Oh, make certain that he dwells in you, for if he does, your heart will not be troubled, neither will it be afraid.

NOTES

1. Now the OMF (Overseas Missionary Fellowship).
2. Henry Francis Lyte (1793–1847), "Abide with Me."
3. From the hymn "How Sweet the Name of Jesus Sounds," by John Newton (1725–1807).
4. J. Hudson Taylor was the founder of the China Inland Mission, now the Overseas Missionary Fellowship.